Manipulation

New technologies are offering companies, politicians, and others unprecedented opportunity to manipulate us. Sometimes we are given the illusion of power – of freedom – through choice, yet the game is rigged, pushing us in specific directions that lead to less wealth, worse health, and weaker democracy. In *Manipulation*, nudge theory pioneer and New York Times bestselling author, Cass Sunstein, offers a new definition of manipulation for the digital age; explains why manipulation is wrong; and shows what we can do about it. He reveals how manipulation compromises freedom and personal agency, while threatening to reduce our wellbeing. He explains the difference between manipulation and unobjectionable forms of influence, including "nudges." And he lifts the lid on manipulation by artificial intelligence, algorithms, and generative AI, as well as threats posed by deepfakes, social media, and "dark patterns," which can trick people into giving up time and money. Drawing on decades of groundbreaking research in behavioral science, this landmark book outlines steps we can take to counteract manipulation in our daily lives and offers guidance to protect consumers, investors, and workers.

Cass R. Sunstein is the Robert Walmsley University Professor at Harvard. The most cited law professor in the world, he is the founder and director of the Program on Behavioral Economics and Public Policy at Harvard Law School. In 2018, he received the Holberg Prize from the government of Norway, sometimes described as the equivalent of the Nobel Prize for law and the humanities. During the Obama Administration, he served as Administrator of the White House Office of Information and Regulatory Affairs. He is author of hundreds of articles and dozens of books, including several *New York Times* bestsellers.

Manipulation
What It Is, Why It's Bad, What To Do About It

Cass R. Sunstein

CAMBRIDGE
UNIVERSITY PRESS

Shaftesbury Road, Cambridge CB2 8EA, United Kingdom

One Liberty Plaza, 20th Floor, New York, NY 10006, USA

477 Williamstown Road, Port Melbourne, VIC 3207, Australia

314–321, 3rd Floor, Plot 3, Splendor Forum, Jasola District Centre, New Delhi – 110025, India

103 Penang Road, #05-06/07, Visioncrest Commercial, Singapore 238467

Cambridge University Press is part of Cambridge University Press & Assessment, a department of the University of Cambridge.

We share the University's mission to contribute to society through the pursuit of education, learning and research at the highest international levels of excellence.

www.cambridge.org
Information on this title: www.cambridge.org/9781009620215

DOI: 10.1017/9781009620222

© Cass R. Sunstein 2025

This publication is in copyright. Subject to statutory exception and to the provisions of relevant collective licensing agreements, no reproduction of any part may take place without the written permission of Cambridge University Press & Assessment.

When citing this work, please include a reference to the DOI 10.1017/9781009620222

First published 2025

Printed in the United Kingdom by CPI Group Ltd, Croydon CR0 4YY

Cover image adapted from images by Evheniia Vasylenko and djvstock respectively, via iStock, Getty Images.

A catalogue record for this publication is available from the British Library

A Cataloging-in-Publication data record for this book is available from the Library of Congress

ISBN 978-1-009-62021-5 Hardback

Cambridge University Press & Assessment has no responsibility for the persistence or accuracy of URLs for external or third-party internet websites referred to in this publication and does not guarantee that any content on such websites is, or will remain, accurate or appropriate.

To Sendhil Mullainathan

CONTENTS

List of Illustrations		*page* ix
List of Tables		x
Preface		xi

Part I: Theory

1	Defining Manipulation	3
2	Evaluating Manipulation	37
3	The Right Not To Be Manipulated	50

Part II: Applications

4	Deepfakes: Manipulated by Technology	71
5	Scarcity and Attention: Manipulated by Sludge	87
6	The Barbie Problem: Manipulated by Social Pressure	106

Part III: The Future

7	Manipulation-Free Nudging, 1	127
8	Manipulation-Free Nudging, 2	144

9	Artificial Intelligence: Promise and Threat	164
	Epilogue: Preventing Theft	196
	Acknowledgments	198
	Index	200

ILLUSTRATIONS

1.1	IndiGo Travel Assistance	page 30
2.1	Eric July online membership	46
2.2	Papa John's cash back	47
3.1	Adobe subscription billing	59
3.2	FDA warning labels, 2011	65
3.3	FDA warning labels, 2019	67
4.1	Deepfakes	72
5.1	SiriusXM cancellation	94
5.2	Air Canada promotional emails	97
6.1	Spotify Fear of Missing Out	111
9.1	EPA Fuel Economy label	180

TABLE

4.1 Social media platforms' policies on manipulated media *page* 84

PREFACE

You need this book.

You might believe that you understand people, but your knowledge barely scratches the surface. True mastery lies in the art of manipulation, a practice as old as humanity itself.

This book is your guide into that forbidden realm, where the rules are rewritten and the stakes are life itself. It will reveal the techniques, the psychology, and the strategies used by the world's most influential figures.

You will learn not just to recognize manipulation but to wield it with precision.

As you turn these pages, let the power of this knowledge sink in. Imagine how your life could change with the ability to influence anyone, anywhere, at any time.

This is more than a book; it is a key to unlocking potential you never knew existed. But be warned – this journey will transform you. Once you embrace these secrets, there is no turning back.

Are you ready to wield the power that has shaped empires and commanded legions? The choice is yours, but remember: with great power comes great responsibility. Welcome to the world of manipulation.

A confession: I didn't write the italicized paragraphs. I asked ChatGPT to write a manipulative start to a book on manipulation, and there we are.[1] I kind of hate those paragraphs, but they're not bad. They promise to disclose secrets. They're an attempted

---

[1] OpenAI, Response to this set of prompts, ChatGPT (June, 2024), https://chatgpt.com/ (enter query into "Message ChatGPT" box). "Write a manipulative start to a book on manipulation"; "Make it nonfiction"; "Make it more manipulative."

seduction. They play on the reader's emotions. *("This is more than a book; it is a key to unlocking potential you never knew existed.")*
    Here is a better-known passage.[2] You know it, don't you?

> *Now the serpent was more crafty than any other wild animal that the LORD God had made. He said to the woman, "Did God say, 'You shall not eat from any tree in the garden'?"*
>
> *The woman said to the serpent, "We may eat of the fruit of the trees in the garden;*
>
> *but God said, 'You shall not eat of the fruit of the tree that is in the middle of the garden, nor shall you touch it, or you shall die.'"*
>
> *But the serpent said to the woman, "You will not die; God knows that when you eat of it your eyes will be opened, and you will be like God, knowing good and evil."*
>
> *So when the woman saw that the tree was good for food, and that it was a delight to the eyes, and that the tree was to be desired to make one wise, she took of its fruit and ate; and she also gave some to her husband, who was with her, and he ate.*
>
> *Then the eyes of both were opened, and they knew that they were naked; and they sewed fig leaves together and made loincloths for themselves.*

    The serpent was a manipulator. He was a seducer. He knew a lot about human psychology. He knew how to play on the emotions of his targets: "your eyes will be opened, and you will be like God." (Was he an expert on optimistic bias? On behavioral science? Obviously.) Actually ChatGPT used some of the same techniques as the serpent. It offered to disclose hidden secrets, and to open readers' eyes.
    We live in an era in which manipulation is pervasive, especially online. A central purpose of manipulation is to attract attention. If a social media company can grab your attention, it might be able to charge advertisers. If an advertiser can grab your attention, it might be able to get your money. Politicians want your money and

---

[2] Genesis 3:1–7.

your vote, and they might be able to manipulate you into doing what they want.

But the ability to manipulate people goes well beyond grabbing attention. Manipulators, often aided by (or consisting of) artificial intelligence, can play on your desires, your hopes, your fears, and your weaknesses. If they know a few things about you, they might know a lot of things about you. They might be able to convince you to think what they want you to think. They might be able to convince you to act as they want you to act. They want your money, and they want your time.

Manipulation is a serious threat to well-functioning markets, which depend on informed choices. Manipulation is also a serious threat to democracy. Perhaps above all, it compromises freedom. It is a threat to our capacity to exercise agency.

There is a great deal of work on coercion and almost as much on lying and deception. Comparatively speaking, manipulation is a neglected topic. One reason may be that the term is hard to define. Another may be its pervasiveness and inevitability. If you turn on a television or go online, you will probably find an effort at manipulation. If one of your family members does not try to manipulate you within the next month, you have an unusual family. Because a clear definition is hard to come by, and because some forms of manipulation are inevitable or innocuous, the topic is unusually challenging. I will be trying to overcome the challenges here. While arguing against manipulation (mostly), I will also be pointing to tools of influence that might well be thought to be both manipulative and bad, but that are in fact neither. We should oppose many forms of manipulation, but we should also know what manipulation is not.

This book comes in three parts. Part I explores theoretical questions: What manipulation is, what is wrong with it, and what might be done about it. It devotes a great deal of attention to autonomy, dignity, and social welfare. It connects coercion, lying, deception, and manipulation (the Four Horsemen of the Apocalypse?), and urges that they raise overlapping questions about freedom. As we shall see, manipulation is a protean concept; it has several faces. We can offer definitions that capture some of what manipulation is, but no definition captures all of what manipulation is. (I am going to fuss a lot over definitional matters; some readers might want to skim Chapter 1 and get to Chapter 2 more quickly.) As we shall see, manipulation is (often) wrong because it invades people's autonomy and offends their dignity. We shall also see that manipulation is (often) wrong because it decreases people's welfare – that is, it makes their lives worse. Much of my own focus is on the effects of manipulation in taking people's time or money.

Part II turns to applications. First, it investigates deepfakes and manipulated media. Deepfakes are a pervasive form of manipulation and they can cause serious harm. Second, Part II explores sludge, often used to manipulate people – as, for example, through the imposition of frictions that make it hard for people to exit from a bad situation. The problem of sludge outruns the problem of manipulation, but sludge is a powerful way of manipulating consumers, investors, patients, students, and others. Third, Part II discusses *goods that people buy but wish did not exist*. People can be maneuvered into situations in which they purchase goods whose existence they dislike or even deplore. As we shall see, this problem raises a set of new questions about manipulation in the current era.

Part III explores the future, or at least some aspects of it. It devotes two chapters to ways of influencing people, or nudging them, that do not involve manipulation. I spend a good deal of space on that issue because the topic of nudging has been central to the work of many governments and private institutions, because it is a keen interest of my own, because there is a lot of confusion out there, and because it is important to get clear on the ethical issues, including the line between nudging and manipulation. Some people think that nudges are manipulative. They can be, but they need not be; I explore that issue in detail. Part III also investigates uses of artificial intelligence. My account here is optimistic. I emphasize the potential of artificial intelligence to help people to counteract an absence of information or behavioral biases. Still, I note that artificial intelligence can produce new and especially harmful forms of manipulation.

As we shall see, manipulation is often (not always) a kind of trickery; it treats people as tools or fools, and as objects rather than subjects. If we keep that point in mind, we will have a good sense of what manipulation is, and why it is wrong. As we shall see, it is wrong for many of the same reasons that coercion is wrong. It is not worse than coercion, but it is bad in a different way. It is more insidious. Manipulators do not treat people with respect. They make it harder for people to make reasoned choices about how to live their lives.

Coercion, lies, deception, and manipulation have a great deal in common: They take things from people without their consent. Manipulation can be a form of theft.

With these points in mind, I shall be proposing a new right, suitable for the current era: A right not to be manipulated. We are going to spend a fair bit of time defining the scope of that right, and some of the discussion will get a bit fussy. Specification of the right is not a simple matter. There should be a *moral* right not to be manipulated. There should be a *legal* right too, but it needs to be defined and limited to the egregious cases, in which real harm is imposed. It is much harder to define a right not to be manipulated than to define a right not to be deceived (and I will have something to say about that as well).

As we shall see, the United States quietly recognized something like a right not to be manipulated on August 12, 2024: "Americans should not be subject to confusing, manipulative, or deceptive practices online."[3] Consider that a Declaration of Independence.

I am acutely aware that I will be swimming against a strong tide. In markets and in politics, individuals and institutions have unprecedented abilities to manipulate people. They also have a strong incentive to do so. Consider social media, which wants your attention, and which can figure out how to lead you down rabbit holes (involving conspiracies, or sports, or motor vehicles, or sex). Some of the most serious threats will undoubtedly seem pretty primitive, and pretty tame, in the near future. New technology, including artificial intelligence (AI), will produce unimaginably effective ways to manipulate people, though science fiction helps trigger the imagination, as we will see.

When I served in the federal government, I was shocked at the sheer number of lies and falsehoods that received public

---

[3] *See* Biden-Harris Administration Launches New Effort to Crack Down on Everyday Headaches and Hassles That Waste Americans' Time and Money (Aug. 12, 2024), www.whitehouse.gov/briefing-room/statements-releases/2024/08/12/fact-sheet-biden-harris-administration-launches-new-effort-to-crack-down-on-everyday-headaches-and-hassles-that-waste-americans-time-and-money/.

attention. It occurred to me: "Whatever might be thought will be said." With respect to technology, it is only a slight exaggeration to say: "Whatever can be used will be used." (The fact that it is an exaggeration is important; consider nuclear weapons.) Genies are rarely put back in their bottles.

Still: Consumers, investors, workers, and citizens of the world, unite; you have nothing to lose but your chains.

Part I
THEORY

1 DEFINING MANIPULATION

In 2012, Facebook's Data Science team decided to conduct an experiment to see whether and how they could affect the emotions of the platform's users.[1] For a week, they altered the feeds of 689,003 Facebook users. Some of the users were exposed to fewer posts with positive words or phrases; some of the users saw fewer posts with negative words or phrases. The question was simple: Would this intervention change the kinds of emotions that Facebook users displayed online? In other words, would the platform see *emotional contagion*?

The answer was clear. Facebook did indeed have power over the emotions of its users. People who were exposed to fewer negative posts ended up making fewer negative posts. People who were exposed to fewer positive posts made fewer positive posts. As the authors put it, "emotions expressed by others on Facebook influence our own emotions, constituting experimental evidence for massive-scale contagion via social networks."

The experiment produced widespread alarm, because people immediately saw the implication: If a social media platform wanted to manipulate the feelings of its users, it could do exactly that. A platform could probably make people feel sadder or angrier, or instead happier or more forgiving.

---

[1] Adam D. I. Kramer et al., Experimental Evidence of Massive-Scale Emotional Contagion Through Social Networks, 111 *PNAS* 8788 (2014), available at www.pnas.org/doi/10.1073/pnas.1320040111.

4 / Manipulation

***

It ranks among the most powerful scenes in the history of television. Don Draper, the charismatic star of *Mad Men*, is charged with producing an advertising campaign for Kodak, which has just invented a new slide projector, with continuous viewing. It operates like a wheel. Using the device to display scenes from a once-happy family (as it happens, his own, which is now broken), Draper tells his potential clients:[2]

> In Greek, "nostalgia" literally means, "the pain from an old wound." It's a twinge in your heart, far more powerful than memory alone. This device isn't a spaceship. It's a time machine. It goes backwards, forwards. It takes us to a place where we ache to go again. It's not called the Wheel. It's called the Carousel. It lets us travel the way a child travels. Around and around, and back home again … to a place where we know we are loved.[3]

The Kodak clients are sold. They cancel their meetings with other companies.

***

In 2018, Cambridge Analytica obtained the personal data of about 87 million Facebook users. It did so by using its app called, "This Is Your Digital Life." The app asked users a set of questions designed to learn something about their personalities. By using the app, people unwittingly gave Cambridge Analytica not only answers to those questions but also permission to obtain access to millions of independent data points, based on their use of the Internet. In other words, those who answered the relevant questions were taken to have "agreed" to allow Cambridge Analytica to track their online behavior. Far more broadly, they gave the company access to a large number of data points involving the online behavior of all of the users' friends on Facebook.

---

[2] *See Mad Men*, Quotes, IMDB, www.imdb.com/title/tt1105057/quotes.
[3] Revealingly, nostalgia actually means "longing for a return home," rather than "pain from an old wound."

With these data points, Cambridge Analytica believed that it had the capacity to engage in "psychological targeting." It used people's online behavior to develop psychological profiles, and then sought to influence their behavior, their attitudes, and their emotions through psychologically informed interventions.

Through those interventions, Cambridge Analytica thought that it could affect people's political choices. According to a former employee of the firm, the goal of the effort was to use what was known about people to build "models to exploit what we knew about them and target their inner demons."[4] Pause over that, if you would. We could easily imagine a similar effort to affect people's consumption choices.

* * *

In 2024, while writing this book, I received an email from "Research Awards." The email announced that one of my recent publications "has been provisionally selected for the 'Best Researcher Award.'" It asked me to click on a link to "submit my profile." It was signed: "Organizing Committee, YST Awards."

The article, by the way, was on the topic of manipulation. Does the Organizing Committee have a sense of humor?

I did not click on the link.

* * *

To understand manipulation, we need to know something about human psychology – about how people judge and decide, and about how we depart from perfect rationality. Consider the following cases:

1. A social media platform uses artificial intelligence (AI) to target its users. The AI learns quickly what videos its users are most likely to click on – whether the videos involve tennis, shoes, climate change, immigration, the latest conspiracy theory, the newest laptops, or certain kinds of sex. The platform's goal is to maximize engagement. Its AI is able to create a personalized

---

[4] Anne Barnhill, How Philosophy Might Contribute to the Practical Ethics of Online Manipulation, in *The Philosophy of Online Manipulation* 49, 50–1 (Fleur Jongepier and Michael Klink eds. 2022).

feed for each user. Some users, including many teenagers, seem to become addicted.
2. A real estate company presents information so as to encourage potential tenants to focus only on monthly price and not on other aspects of the deal, including the costs of electricity service, water, repairs, and monthly upkeep. The latter costs are very high.
3. A parent tries to convince an adult child to visit him in a remote area in California, saying, "After all, I'm your father, and I raised you for all those years, and it wasn't always a lot of fun for me – and who knows whether I'm going to live a lot longer?"
4. A hotel near a beach advertises its rooms as costing "just $200 a night!" It does not add that guests must also pay a "resort fee," a "cleaning fee," and a "beach fee," which add up to an additional $90 per night. (There are also taxes.)
5. In an effort to discourage people from smoking, a government requires cigarette packages to contain graphic, frightening health warnings depicting people with life-threatening illnesses.
6. In a campaign advertisement, a political candidate displays ugly photographs of his opponent, set against the background of terrifying music. An announcer reads quotations that, while accurate and not misleading, are taken out of context to make the opponent look at once ridiculous and scary.
7. In an effort to convince consumers to switch to its new, high-cost credit card, a company emphasizes its very low "teaser rate," by which consumers can enjoy low-cost borrowing for a short period. In its advertisement, it depicts happy, elegant, energized people, displaying their card and their new purchases.
8. To reduce pollution (including greenhouse gas emissions), a city requires public utilities to offer clean energy sources as the default providers, subject to opt-out if customers want to save money.

Which of these are manipulative? And why?

Coercion

To answer these questions, we need to make some distinctions. Let us begin with coercion, understood to involve the threatened or actual application of force. If the law forbids you to buy certain medicines without a prescription, and if you would face penalties if you violate that law, coercion is in play. If the police will get involved if you are not wearing your seatbelt, we are speaking of coercion, not manipulation. If you are told that you will be fined or imprisoned if you do not get automobile insurance, you are being coerced.

Note that it is false to say that when coercion is involved, people "have no alternative but to comply." People do have alternatives. They can pay a fine, or go to jail, or attempt to flee.

It is often said that government has a monopoly on the legitimate use of force, which means that in a certain sense, coercion is the province of government and law. But we might want to understand coercion a bit more broadly. If your employer tells you that you will be fired if you do not work on Saturdays, we can fairly say that in an important respect, you have been coerced. If a thief says, "your money or your life," we can fairly say that you have been coerced to give up your money. A reference to "coercion," in cases of this kind, is unobjectionable so long as we know what we are talking about.

Coercion is usually *transparent* and *blunt*. No trickery is involved, and no one is being fooled. Coercion typically depends on transparency.

What is wrong with coercion? That is, of course, a large question. Often coercion is unobjectionable. If you are forbidden from murdering people, or from stealing from them, you have been coerced, but there is no reasonable ground for complaint. People do not have a right to kill or to steal. If you are forbidden to speak freely, or to pray as you think best, we can say that the prohibition offends a fundamental right.

Paternalistic coercion raises its own questions. Suppose that people are forced to buckle their seatbelts, wear motorcycle helmets, or eat healthier foods. Many people object to paternalistic coercion on the ground that choosers know best about what is good for them – about what fits with their preferences, their desires, and their values. Even if they do not know best, they can learn from their own errors. Maybe people have a right to err; maybe they are entitled to be the authors of the narratives of their own lives. These points bear on what manipulation is and why it is wrong; I will return to them.

Lies

Lies may not coerce anyone. "This product will cure baldness" says a marketer, who knows full well that the product will do nothing of the kind. But what is a lie? According to Arnold Isenberg, summarizing many efforts, "A lie is a statement made by one who does not believe it with the intention that someone else shall be led to believe it."[5] Isenberg adds: "The essential parts of the lie, according to our definition, are three. (1) A statement – and we may or may not wish to divide this again into two parts, a proposition and an utterance. (2) A disbelief or a lack of belief on the part of the speaker. (3) An intention on the part of the speaker."

The definition is helpfully specific and narrow. Ordinarily we understand liars to know that what they are saying is false and to be attempting to get others to believe the falsehood. According to a similar account by Thomas Carson, "a lie is a deliberate false statement that the speaker warrants to be true."[6]

Here is a vivid example from John Rawls, speaking of his experience during World War II:[7]

> One day a Lutheran Pastor came up and during his service gave a brief sermon in which he said that God aimed our bullets at the Japanese while God protected us from theirs. I don't know why this made me so angry, but it certainly did. I upbraided the Pastor (who was a First Lieutenant) for saying what I assumed he knew perfectly well – Lutheran that he was – were simply falsehoods without divine provenance. What reason could he possibly have for his trying to comfort the troops? Christian doctrine should not be used for that, though I knew perfectly well it was.

I think I know why the Pastor's sermon made Rawls so angry. The Pastor was not treating the troops respectfully. Actually he was treating them with contempt. Even worse, he was using Christian doctrine in bad faith. He was using what he said to be

---

[5] *See* Arnold Isenberg, Deontology and the Ethics of Lying, 24 *Philosophy and Phenomenological Research* 463, 466 (1964).
[6] *See* Thomas L. Carson, *Lying and Deception* 15 (2010).
[7] John Rawls, *A Brief Inquiry into the Meaning of Sin and Faith* (2009).

God's will, but did not believe to be God's will, in order to make people feel better. That is a form of fraud. It is horrific. It is a desecration.

Inadvertent falsehoods belong in an altogether different category. If you say, "climate change is not real," and if that is what you think, you are not lying, even if what you say is false. You might be reckless or you might be negligent, but you are not lying.

It is noteworthy that the standard definition of lying does not include false statements from people with various cognitive and emotional problems, who may sincerely believe what they are saying. In the 1960s, my father had a little construction company and he worked near a mental hospital. He was often visited by someone who lived there, who would give my father a large check and say, "Mr. Sunstein, here's a check for you. I have enough funds to cover it. Will this be enough for the day?"

It is fair to say that while my father's visitor was not telling the truth, he was not exactly lying. We would not respond to my father's benefactor with the same anger that Rawls felt toward the Pastor.

Or consider the case of confabulators, defined as people with memory disorders who fill in gaps with falsehoods, not knowing that they are false. Nor does the definition include people who believe what they say because of motivated reasoning. People often believe what they want to believe, even if it is untrue, and people whose beliefs are motivated may not be liars. They might be motivated to say that they are spectacularly successful, and while that might not be true, they might not be lying, because they believe what they say. They might say, "My company is bound to make huge profits in the next year," not because there is any evidence to support their optimistic prediction, but because they wish the statement to be true. Such people might be spreading falsehoods, but if they do not know that what they are spreading is false, it does not seem right to describe them as "lying."

Deception

Now turn to deception. It is often said that the term is broader than "lying." On a standard definition, it refers to *intentionally causing other people to hold false beliefs*. You might deceive people into holding a false belief without making a false statement. You might sell a new "natural pain medication" to willing buyers, referring truthfully to the testimony of "dozens of satisfied customers," even though there is no evidence that the pain medication does anyone any good. You might sell an airline ticket to a beautiful location, stating that the ticket costs "just $199," without mentioning that the ticket comes with an assortment of extra fees, leading to a total cost of $299. You might sell your house to a naïve buyer, emphasizing that it has not been necessary to make any repairs over the last ten years, even though it is clear that the house will need plenty of repairs over the next six months. In all of these cases, you have deceived people without lying.[8]

What is wrong with lying and deception? (For present purposes, we can group them together.) They are often taken to be illicit forms of influence. Return to Rawls' Pastor, who treated the soldiers disrespectfully. Much of the time, liars and deceivers are thieves. They try to take things from people (their money, their time, their vote, their sympathy) without their consent.

Still, we have to be careful here. It is widely though not universally[9] agreed that some lies are acceptable or perhaps even mandatory. A few decades ago, my father started to stumble on the tennis court. My mother and I brought him to the hospital for various tests. After conferring with the doctor, my mother came to my father's hospital room to announce, "I have great news. They didn't discover anything serious. They will keep you here for another day, out of an excess of caution, but basically, you're fine!"

When my mother took me downstairs, to drive me back to law school, her face turned ashen. She said, "Your father has a brain tumor, and there's nothing they can do about it. He has about a year. But I'm not going to tell him, and you're not, either."

---

[8] *See* Schlomo Cohen, Manipulation and Deception, 96 *Australasian Journal of Philosophy* 483 (2018).
[9] *See* Carson, *supra* note 6, for a good discussion of why absolutist or near-absolutist positions do not work; Sissela Bok, *Lying: Moral Choice in Public and Private Life* (1999); for a discussion of absolutist or near-absolutist positions with respect to lies and lying; *see also*, Christine M. Korsgaard, What's Wrong With Lying?, in *Philosophical Inquiry: Classic and Contemporary Readings* (Jonathan E. Adler and Catherine Z. Elgin eds. 2007), for what is easily taken as a near-absolute ban on lying, on Kantian grounds.

Was she wrong to lie to him? I don't know. Was Bill Clinton wrong to lie to the American people about his relationship with Monica Lewinsky? I believe so, but not everyone agrees.[10]

Consider the following propositions:

1. If an armed thief comes to your door and asks you where you keep your money, you are entitled to lie.
2. If a terrorist captures a spy and asks her to give up official secrets, she is under no obligation to tell the truth.
3. If you tell your children that Santa Claus is coming on the night before Christmas, you have not done anything wrong.
4. If you compliment your spouse on his appearance, even though he is not looking especially good, it would be pretty rigid to say that you have violated some ethical stricture.

We should conclude that lies and deception are generally wrong, and I will have something to say about why. But they are not always wrong.

Meaning and Morality

A great deal of effort has been devoted to the definition of manipulation, almost exclusively within the philosophical literature.[11] Most of those efforts are both instructive and honorable, and I will build on them here. In the end, it might be doubted that a single definition will exhaust the territory. I will be offering two quite different accounts (one in this chapter and one in Chapter 6), and there are others.

Let us begin with some methodological remarks. On one account, defining manipulation is an altogether different enterprise from explaining why and when manipulation is wrong. We might say that manipulation occurs in certain situations and then make an independent judgment about when or whether it is wrong. We might conclude that it is presumptively wrong, or almost always wrong, because of what it means or does. Or we might think that it is often

---

[10] *See* Thomas Nagel, Concealment and Exposure, 27 *Phil & Pub Affairs* 3 (1998).
[11] An excellent overview is Christian Coons and Michael Webster eds. *Manipulation: Theory and Practice* (2014). Also superb is Robert Noggle, *The Ethics of Manipulation* (2018); *Stanford Encyclopedia of Philosophy*, available at https://plato.stanford.edu/entries/ethics-manipulation/.

justified – if, for example, it is necessary to increase public safety or improve public health.

On another account, manipulation is a "thick" or "moralized" concept, in the sense that it always carries with it a normative evaluation. Compare the words "generous," "brave," "kind," and "cruel"; any definition of these words must be accompanied with a positive or negative evaluation. To say that an act is "generous" is to say that it is good. You might think that to say that an act is "manipulative" is to say that it is bad.

In my view, the first account is right, and it is the right way to proceed. A manipulative act might be good. You might manipulate your spouse in order to reduce serious health risks that she faces. A doctor might manipulate a patient for the same reason. True, you might say, in such cases, that manipulation is pro tanto wrong, or presumptively wrong, and that like coercion, deception, or lying, a pro tanto wrong or a presumptive wrong might ultimately be right (and perhaps morally mandatory). But we can, I think, define manipulation before offering a judgment about when and whether it is right or wrong. In any case, that is the strategy that I will be pursuing here. And my own preferred definitions in this chapter, intended not to be exhaustive but to capture a set of important cases of manipulation, will turn out to embed something like an account of why manipulation is presumptively wrong.

The task of definition presents other puzzles. When we insist that "deception" means this, and that "manipulation" means that, what exactly are we saying? Are we trying to capture people's intuitions? Are we trying to capture ordinary usage? What if intuitions or usages diverge? Are we seeking to capture the views of the majority? If so, are we asking an *empirical* question, to be resolved through empirical methods? What would those methods look like? Can artificial intelligence help? More broadly: When people (including philosophers) disagree about what manipulation means, what exactly are they disagreeing about?

I suggest that when we try to define a term like manipulation, we are engaging in something like interpretation in Ronald Dworkin's sense.[12] In Dworkin's account, interpretation involves

---

[12] *See* Ronald Dworkin, *Law's Empire* (1985).

two steps. First, an interpreter must "fit" the existing materials. To say that Shakespeare's *Hamlet* is a play about cooking or fishing would be implausible, because any such interpretation does not fit the materials. It does not map onto the play. Second, an interpreter must, within the constraints of fit, "justify" the materials – that is, must make the best possible sense out of them. To say that *Hamlet* is a play about the evils of the welfare state would not only fail to fit the play; it would also make little sense of it. To say that *Hamlet* is about an Oedipal conflict is interesting and perhaps more than that.

Dworkin is speaking of interpretation in many domains, above all law, but I think that his understanding can be adapted for our purposes here. For a term like manipulation, existing understandings constrain possible definitions. We can imagine definitions that are palpably wrong, or that are far too narrow or far too broad. They are wrong, or too narrow or too broad, because they do not fit ordinary usage. A definition of manipulation that is limited to inducing guilt is both too narrow and too broad. A definition that includes reasoned persuasion is too broad. When people, including philosophers, debate what manipulation is, they are often debating what fits ordinary usage.

Within the category of definitions that are not palpably wrong, and that are not clearly too narrow or too broad, some possible definitions turn out to produce a click of recognition or assent, in the sense that they appear to make good sense, or best sense, of our intuitions or our usage. We might think that on reflection one candidate best specifies what manipulation really is, as we use that term. When people, including philosophers, debate the best definition of manipulation, they are often debating what makes the most sense of our intuitions or our usage. I am aware that these are brief remarks on a complicated topic; they are meant to signal the approach that I will be following here.

Tools and Fools

Manipulation is frequently distinguished from rational persuasion on the one hand and coercion on the other; it might be described as a third way of influencing people. If you persuade someone to buy a particular car, by giving them good reasons to believe that it will best suit their needs, you are not manipulating them. There is also a disputed relationship between deception and manipulation. Suppose that a politician uses emotionally gripping imagery in an effort to convince voters that if they vote for his opponent the country will essentially come to an end. We can easily characterize that as a case of manipulation. But it might also be seen as one of deception insofar as the politician is seeking to induce false beliefs. If we look carefully at what manipulators are doing, we will often discover that they are seeking to induce such beliefs in the people they are manipulating. That is one reason that some people deny that there is a clear or simple distinction between deception and manipulation.

I asked ChatGPT to define manipulation (prompt "Define Manipulation," August 3, 2024), and here is what it came up with:

> Manipulation refers to the act of skillfully controlling or influencing someone or something, often in a deceptive or underhanded way, to achieve a desired outcome. It can occur in various contexts, such as interpersonal relationships, politics, or media, and is usually characterized by the use of tactics that exploit emotions, perceptions, or situations to gain advantage or control over others.

That is a reasonable start. It does have the disadvantage of conflating manipulation with deception ("often in a deceptive or underhanded way"), and the word "often" introduces vagueness. Among philosophers, some of the most promising definitional efforts focus specifically on the effects of manipulation *in counteracting or undermining people's ability to engage in rational deliberation*. And indeed, that will be my principal emphasis here. On T. M. Wilkinson's account, for example, manipulation "is a kind of influence that bypasses or subverts the target's rational capacities."[13] Wilkinson urges that manipulation "subverts and insults a person's autonomous decision making," in a way that treats its objects as "tools and fools."[14] He thinks that "manipulation is intentionally

---

[13] T. M. Wilkinson, Nudging and Manipulation, 61 *Political Studies* 341, 342 (2013).
[14] Wilkinson, *supra* note 13, at 145.

and successfully influencing someone using methods that pervert choice."[15]

The idea here is close to that of deception, but it is not the same. The idea of "perverting" choice is broader than that of "inducing false beliefs." I have said that many acts of manipulation do that, but you can manipulate people without inducing any such beliefs. Manipulative statements or actions might be deceptive, but they need not be. My mother did not much like my father's parents and she did not want to visit them. She and my father lived in Waban, Massachusetts, and my grandparents lived far away, in Pittsburgh, Pennsylvania. Trying to get my mother to agree to visit, my grandmother said to her, "You really should visit us. We'll probably die soon." My mother felt manipulated, and after getting off the phone, exclaimed to my father and me, "She keeps promising!" My grandparents lived for a very long time, but my grandmother was not seeking to deceive my mother.

Consider, for example, efforts to enlist attractive people to sell cars, or to use frightening music and ugly photos to attack a political opponent. We might think that in such cases, customers and voters are being insulted in the sense that the relevant speaker is not giving them anything like a straightforward account of the virtues of the car or the vices of the opponent, but is instead using associations of various kinds to press the chooser in the manipulator's preferred direction. On a plausible view, manipulation is involved to the extent that it bypasses or distorts, and does not respect, people's capacity to reflect and deliberate. Here again, it is important to notice that we should speak of degrees of manipulation, rather than a simple on–off switch.

Ruth Faden and Tom Beauchamp define psychological manipulation as "any intentional act that successfully influences a

---

[15] *See ibid.* An especially valuable discussion, reaching a different conclusion, is Anne Barnhill, What is Manipulation? in *Manipulation: Theory and Practice* 50, 72 (Christian Coons and Michael Weber eds. 2014). Note the emphasis, in defining manipulation, on the manipulator's attempt to influence choices and decisions. If one tries to put people in a certain mood (for example, by taking them to lunch), manipulation is not involved if there is no effort to influence their choices, even when the attempt to lift their mood does not involve an appeal to their reflective and deliberative capacities. (Indeed, the most successful efforts to lift moods often make no such appeal.)

person to belief or behavior by causing changes in mental processes *other than those involved in understanding*."[16] Joseph Raz suggests that "Manipulation, unlike coercion, does not interfere with a person's options. Instead it perverts the way that person reaches decisions, forms preferences or adopts goals."[17] Alan Wood offers a generalization, to the effect that "when getting others to do is morally problematic, this is not so much because you are making them worse off (less happy, less satisfied) but, instead, it is nearly always because you are messing with their *freedom* – whether by taking it away, limiting it, usurping it, or subverting it."[18] The idea of "messing with freedom" is helpful; victims of manipulation often feel messed with in that way.

Moti Gorin argues that manipulators typically "intend their manipulees to behave in ways they (the manipulators) do not believe to be supported by reasons."[19] On another account, "manipulation is hidden influence. Or more fully, manipulating someone means intentionally and covertly influencing their decision-making, by targeting and exploiting their decision-making vulnerabilities. Covertly influencing someone – imposing a hidden influence – means influencing them in a way they aren't consciously aware of, and in a way they couldn't easily become aware of were they to try and understand what was impacting their decision-making process."[20]

Of course, the idea of "perverting" choice, or people's way of reaching decisions or forming preferences, is not self-defining; it can be understood to refer to methods that do not appeal to, or produce, the right degree or kind of reflective deliberation. If so, an objection to manipulation is that it "infringes upon the autonomy of the victim by subverting and insulting their decision-making powers."[21] Note that

---

[16] Ruth Faden and Tom Beauchamp, *A History and Theory of Informed Consent* 354–68 (1986) (emphasis added).
[17] Joseph Raz, *The Morality of Freedom* 377–9 (1988).
[18] Alan Wood, Coercion, Manipulation, Exploitation, in *Manipulation: Theory and Practice* 17, 17–18 (Christian Coons and Michael Weber eds. 2014) (emphasis added).
[19] Mori Gorin, *Toward a Theory of Interpersonal Manipulation* (2014).
[20] Daniel Susser, Beat Roessler, and Helen Nissenbaum, Technology, Autonomy, and Manipulation, 8 *Internet Policy Review* (June 2019), at 4.
[21] See Wilkinson, *supra* note 13.

undue complexity can be a form of manipulation, because it subverts and insults people's decision-making powers.[22]

That objection also offers one account of what is wrong with lies, which attempt to alter behavior not by engaging people on the merits and asking them to decide accordingly, but by enlisting falsehoods, usually in the service of the liar's goals (an idea that also points the way to a welfarist account of what usually makes lies wrong[23]). A lie is disrespectful to its objects, not least if it attempts to exert influence without asking people to make a deliberative choice in light of relevant facts. But when lies are not involved, and when the underlying actions appear to be manipulative, the challenge is to concretize the ideas of "subverting" and "insulting."[24]

Trickery, Influence, and Choice

Consider a simple definition, to this effect:

1. Manipulation is a form of trickery that does not respect its victim's capacity for reflective and deliberative choice.

That definition certainly captures many cases of manipulation. It should be clear that manipulation is meant to affect thought or action, or both, and so we might amend the definition in this way:

2. Manipulation is a form of trickery, intended to affect thought or action (or both), that does not respect its victim's capacity for reflective and deliberative choice.

Definitions (1) and (2) do not by any means exhaust the territory, but for purposes of policy and law, they are useful. They get at a key issue with manipulation, which is that it compromises people's capacity for agency. Note that the word "trickery" is helpful

---

[22] *See* Petra Persson, Attention Manipulation and Information Overload, 2 *Behavioral Public Policy* 78 (2018).

[23] Of course, some lies are justified; the intentions of the liar might matter (for example, to spare someone's feelings), and the consequences might be exculpatory (to prevent serious harm).

[24] For relevant discussion in the context of deception, *see* Richard Craswell, Interpreting Deceptive Advertising, 65 *BU Law Review* 657 (1985); Richard Craswell, Regulating Deceptive Advertising: The Role of Cost-Benefit Analysis, 64 *Southern California Law Review* 549 (1991).

in order to distinguish manipulation from coercion, lies, and deception.[25] If it is objected that lies and deception can also count as trickery, we might try a more unwieldy formulation, amending (1):

3. Manipulation is a form of trickery, not involving lies and deception, that does not respect its victim's capacity for reflective and deliberative choice.

We could combine (2) and (3):

4. Manipulation is a form of trickery, intended to affect thought or action (or both) and not involving lies and deception, that does not respect its victim's capacity for reflective and deliberative choice.

In my view, (4) is a valuable definition of a widespread kind of manipulation. But unwieldiness is not ideal, and definition (1) captures much of ordinary usage while also, I suggest, making good sense of that ordinary usage.

I emphasize that none of the foregoing definitions captures all forms of manipulation. In my view, there is no unified account of manipulation. Some kinds of manipulation do not involve trickery at all. If I make someone feel guilty in order to get them to do what I want ("I will be just devastated if you do not go to my birthday

---

[25] Robert Noggle, Pressure, Trickery, and a Unified Account of Manipulation, 57 *American Philosophical Quarterly* 241, 242 (2020). Noggle offers a superb discussion of trickery but concludes that it is underinclusive. I agree that it is underinclusive but do not think that pressure, which he emphasizes, is a form of manipulation. Urging a Mistake Account, Noggle says this: "It appears, then, that manipulative pressure can only succeed when the target mistakenly chooses the lesser good. Consequently, manipulative pressure and trickery-based manipulation are not so different after all. Both are attempts to influence the target's behavior by getting her to make a mistake. Trickery-based manipulation involves attempting to get the target to adopt a mistaken belief, desire, emotion, or other mental state. Manipulative pressure attempts to get the target to respond akratically to an incentive or disincentive in a way that is disproportionate to its actual magnitude. Thus, the mistake made by the target of successful manipulative pressure consists in akratically responding to the manipulator's incentive or disincentive as though its magnitude were much larger than it really is." I will not discuss this intriguing account in any detail, but I would be cautious about connecting the idea of manipulation with the production of mistakes, because manipulators can prevent mistakes, rather than induce them. But it would be possible to understand the ideas of mistakes to include process as well as outcomes, in which case a Mistake Account might start to converge with my own.

party"), I might not be tricking them, but I might well be manipulating them. If I make things very complicated, so as to prevent people from fully understanding the situation and to lead them to make the choice I want, I may or may not be tricking them, but I am certainly manipulating them.[26]

We might broaden definition (1) in this way:

5. Manipulation is a form of influence that does not respect its victim's capacity for reflective and deliberative choice.

This definition has the advantage of including cases that do not involve trickery. It has the disadvantage of potentially excessive breadth. If you condescend to people, and treat them as children, you are not respecting their capacity for reflective and deliberative choice. But you are not necessarily manipulating them. We might take (5) as capturing cases of manipulation that (1) does not include, while acknowledging that (5) is a bit too broad.

We could, of course, amend (5) in a way that fits with (2), (3), or (4), as in:

6. Manipulation is a form of influence, intended to affect thought or action (or both), that does not respect its victim's capacity for reflective and deliberative choice.
7. Manipulation is a form of influence, not involving lies or deception, that does not respect its victim's capacity for reflective and deliberative choice.
8. Manipulation is a form of influence, intended to affect thought or action (or both), and not involving lies or deception, that does not respect its victim's capacity for reflective and deliberative choice.

I suggest that definition (8) captures many (not all) cases of manipulation, and although it is a bit too broad, it gets at a lot of the cases that should concern those involved in policy and law. For purposes of policy and law, definition (8) may be the best we can do (though again it does not capture all of the territory, see Chapter 6).

To understand manipulation in any of the foregoing ways, it should not be necessary to make controversial claims about the nature of choice or the role of emotions. We should agree that many

---

[26] *See* Persson, *supra* note 22.

decisions are based on unconscious processing and that people often lack a full sense of the wellsprings of their own choices.[27] Even if this is so, a manipulator might impose some kind of influence that does not respect people's capacity for reflection and deliberation. It is possible to acknowledge the view that emotions might themselves be judgments of value[28] while also emphasizing that manipulators attempt to influence people's choices without respecting their capacity to engage in reflective thinking about the values at stake. In ordinary language, the idea of manipulation is invoked by people who are not committed to controversial views about psychological or philosophical questions, and it is best to understand that idea in a way that brackets the relevant controversies.

Is manipulation, so understood, less bad than coercion? Some people think that there is a kind of continuum here, with manipulation being less intrusive or severe. But the two are qualitatively distinct, and each is bad, when it is bad, in its own way. As Christian Coons and Michael Weber put it, "While it may be more frustrating and frightening to be ruled by a Genghis Khan (as typically characterized) or Joseph Stalin than by a David Koresh or some other cult leader, there may be an important sense . . . in which the latter involves a much more regrettable loss of dignity and, perhaps, our very selves."[29]

Manipulating System 1

We can make progress in understanding some kinds of manipulation with reference to the now-widespread view that the human mind contains not one but two "cognitive systems."[30] In the social science literature, the two systems are described as System 1 and System 2.[31] System 1 is the automatic, intuitive system, prone to biases and to the use of heuristics, understood as mental shortcuts or rules of thumb. System 2 is more deliberative, calculative, and reflective. Manipulators often target System 1, and they attempt

---

[27] *See* Daniel Kahneman, *Thinking, Fast and Slow* (2011).
[28] *See* Martha Nussbaum, *Upheavals of Thought* (2003).
[29] Coons and Weber, *supra* note 11, at 16.
[30] Kahneman, *supra* note 27; Timothy Wilson, *Strangers to Ourselves* (2014).
[31] *See* Kahneman, *supra* note 27.

to bypass or undermine System 2. A graphic warning might, for example, get your emotions going; it might promote fear, whether or not there is anything to be scared of. The prospect of riches (for buying, say, a lottery ticket) might promote hope and optimism, even if your chances are vanishingly small.

System 1 works quickly. Much of the time, it is on automatic pilot. It is driven by habits. When it hears a loud noise, it is inclined to run. It can be lustful. It is full of appetite. When it is offended, it wants to hit back. It certainly eats a delicious brownie. It can procrastinate; it can be impulsive. It is easy to manipulate. It wants what it wants when it wants it. It can be excessively fearful. It can become hysterical. It can be too complacent. It is a doer, not a planner.

By contrast, System 2 is reflective and deliberative. It calculates. It hears a loud noise, and it assesses whether the noise is a cause for concern. It thinks about probability, carefully though sometimes slowly. It does not really get offended. If it sees reasons for offense, it makes a careful assessment of what, all things considered, ought to be done. It sees a delicious brownie and it makes a judgment about whether, all things considered, it should eat it. It is harder to manipulate. It is committed to the idea of self-control. It is a planner more than a doer.

At this point, you might well ask: What, exactly, are these systems? Do they refer to anything physical? In the brain? The best answer is that the idea of two systems should be seen as a heuristic device, a simplification that is designed to refer to automatic, effortless processing and more complex, effortful processing. If a seller of a product triggers an automatic reaction of terror or hope, System 1 is the target; if a seller of a product attempts to persuade people that the product will save them money over the period of a decade, System 2 is the target. That is sufficient for my purposes here. But it is also true that identifiable regions of the brain are active in different tasks, and hence it may well be right to suggest that the idea of "systems" has physical referents. An influential discussion states that "[a]utomatic and controlled processes can be roughly distinguished by where they occur in the brain."[32]

---

[32] Colin Camerer et al., Neuroeconomics: How Neuroscience Can Inform Economics, 43 *Journal Economic Literature* 1, 17 (2005).

We need not venture contested claims about the brain, or the nature of the two systems, in order to find it helpful to suggest that many actions count as manipulative because they appeal to System 1, and because System 2 is being subverted, tricked, undermined, or insufficiently involved or not informed. Consider the case of subliminal advertising, which should be deemed manipulative because it operates "behind the back" of the people involved, without appealing to their conscious awareness. If subliminal advertising works, people's decisions are affected in a way that does not respect their deliberative capacities. If this is the defining problem with subliminal advertising, we can understand why involuntary hypnosis (supposing it is possible) would also count as manipulative. But almost no one favors subliminal advertising, and, to say the least, the idea of involuntary hypnosis lacks much appeal. One question is whether admittedly taboo practices can shed light on actions that are more familiar or that might be able to command broader support.

The larger point is that an understanding of System 1 and System 2 helps explain why manipulation, as defined in (1) through (8) above, is often successful. The relevant trickery, or form of influence, targets System 1 or overwhelms System 2.

Falling Short of Ideals

In an illuminating discussion, drawing on Noggle's defining work,[33] Anne Barnhill offers a distinctive account. She defines manipulation[34] as "directly influencing someone's beliefs, desires, or emotions such that she falls short of ideals for belief, desire, or emotion in ways typically not in her self-interest or likely not in her self-interest in the present context."

You can see that account as consistent with the central understandings in my various definitions. For example, trickery that does not respect people's capacity for reflective and deliberative

---

[33] Robert Noggle, Manipulative Actions: A Conceptual and Moral Analysis, 34 *American Philosophical Quarterly* 57 (1995).
[34] Barnhill, *supra* note 15, at 72. Barnhill builds on the pioneering, superb treatment in Noggle, *supra* note 33.

choice is a form of influence that causes people to fall short of relevant ideals for belief, desire, or emotion.

But Barnhill's definition is broader than those I have offered, and that is an advantage. You can directly influence someone's beliefs, desires, or emotions, leading them to fall short of relevant ideals, without engaging in trickery. You can manipulate someone into falling short of ideals for (say) gratitude, romantic love, or anger, even if we are not dealing with a situation that calls for reflective or deliberative choice. Consider flirting, which may or may not be manipulative. Sometimes it is; sometimes it is not. Whether it should be counted as manipulative is illuminatingly answered by reference to Barnhill's definition. As she says, "Flirting influences someone by causing changes in mental processes other than those involved in understanding, but flirting isn't manipulative in all cases."[35] Maybe the flirt is inducing certain feelings, but maybe those feelings are entirely warranted. (She's funny, and she's fun.) Maybe there is no manipulation at all (and reflection and deliberation may not be involved). Whether flirting is manipulative plausibly depends on *whether the person with whom the flirt is flirting is being influenced in ways that cause him to have beliefs, desires, or emotions that fall short of the relevant ideals.* (If she doesn't much like him, and is just trying to get him to do something for her, she is manipulating him.)

Inducing emotions need not, but can, be a form of manipulation. Shakespeare's Iago was a master manipulator, trying to produce anger. There are ideals for becoming angry and they can be violated. You can be manipulated to become angry or indignant. You probably have been. The android Anya, in the 2014 movie *Ex Machina*, was terrific at manipulating people, or at least one person, into feeling romantic love (see Chapter 8). You can fall short of ideals for falling in love. In general, the idea of "falling short of ideals" is exceedingly helpful.

Note that the standard here is best taken as objective, not subjective. The question is whether someone has, in fact, fallen short of ideals. Still, there is a problem with Barnhill's definition, which is that it excludes, from the category of manipulation, influences that

[35] Barnhill, *supra* note 15.

are in the self-interest of the person who is being influenced. Some acts of manipulation count as such even if they leave the object of the influence a lot better off. You might be manipulated to purchase a car that you end up much enjoying. You might be manipulated into exercising self-control – not smoking, not drinking alcohol, not drinking a diet cola. We might be willing to say that such acts are justified, especially if we are focused on human welfare – but they are manipulative all the same.

Note also that the breadth of Barnhill's definition is a vice as well as a virtue. It seems to pick up lying and deception as well as manipulation. Perhaps we could amend the definition so as to exclude them. My own definition captures a subset of what Barnhill's does; I suggest only that it is an important subset. And as we will see in Chapter 6, there are forms of manipulation that outrun Barnhill's definition.

A Complication: Properly Nondeliberative Decisions

Consider this: A teenage girl is starring in a school play. The play is being performed in a place and at a time that is worse than inconvenient for her mother. When her mother tells her that she is not coming, the girl starts to cry. She says, through her tears, "This is really important to me, and all the other parents will be there!"

Is the daughter manipulating her mother?

Maybe not. A reflective and deliberative choice, on the mother's part, depends partly on the effects of her decision on her daughter, and the intense and emotional reaction, if it is sincere, is informative on that count. The daughter has not engaged in a form of trickery that fails to respect her mother's capacity for reflective and deliberative choice. If you are deciding whether to do something that matters to people who matter to you, you should consider the emotional impact of the decision on *them* – and if they act in a way that produces an emotional effect on *you*, they might be informing you; they might not be manipulating you. As Noggle puts it, "Moral persuasion often appeals to emotions like empathy or to invitations to imagine how it would feel to be treated the way one proposes to treat someone else. Such forms of moral persuasion – at least when they are sincere – do not seem manipulative even though they appeal as much to emotion as to reason."[36] He adds, "Nor does it seem manipulative to induce someone to feel more fearful of something whose actual dangers that person has underestimated."

In short, some decisions are *properly nondeliberative*, which identifies an important reason why definitions (1) through (8) are not exhaustive, and why Barnhill's definition picks up an important kind of manipulation – as, for example, when people are induced to feel anger or guilt when they really should not. Recall that Shakespeare's Iago was a manipulator, and he was a master at producing emotional reactions. So we should indeed say, with Noggle and Barnhill, that *manipulation can occur if people are directly influencing someone's desires or emotions such that they fall short of ideals for having those desires or emotions.*

In the case of the teenage girl and the school play, it is important to know the daughter's state of mind. Is she feigning those tears? Is she exaggerating her emotional reaction to get her mother to come? If so, she is being deceptive, and she is also engaged in manipulation. She is making her mother think something that is not true (to the effect that she is devastated at the thought of her mother's not showing up), and she is manipulating her to have an emotional reaction that is not justified by the situation. This is the problem to which both Barnhill and Noggle rightly draw attention. It shows that people can be manipulated in contexts that involve properly nondeliberative decisions.

---

[36] Noggle, *supra* note 25. Noggle presents his view in detail in Robert Noggle, *Manipulation: Its Nature, Mechanisms, and Moral Status* (2025). His book is extraordinarily good, and I have learned a great deal from it (as well as from his prior work). He develops what he calls Mistake Account of manipulation, summarized in this way: "Manipulation is an influence that operates by inducing the target to make a mistake." It should be clear that I do not accept this account. My own view is that there is no unified account of manipulation, and that the account on which I mainly rely on in this chapter, pointing to a kind of trickery that does not respect people's capacity to make reflective and deliberative choices, is essential but incomplete. Noggle has a lot to say in favor of what he called the Trickery Account; he likes a lot about it but believes that it misses what is captured by a Pressure Account of manipulation. In my view, pressure is something real and important, but it is not manipulation. I also think that manipulation can occur even if it leads people to correct decisions, rather than to mistakes; consider a doctor who manipulates a patient to have a necessary operation. But nothing said here does justice to Noggle's discussion, and I refer readers to it, with admiration and enthusiasm.

If you are deciding whether to fall in love, you can be manipulated – by, let's say, a rogue or a seducer. But your decision, if it is a decision at all, might not be, and perhaps should not be, a reflective and deliberative choice. You feel it, or you do not. If you fall in love with someone who is amazing in relevant ways, manipulation need not be involved, even if your falling in love does not involve reflection and deliberation; try the 1990 novel *Possession*, by A. S. Byatt, for a transporting example. But if you fall in love with someone who knows how to press your buttons, you are being manipulated. A lot of fiction is about that problem; try the 1915 novel *Of Human Bondage*, by William Somerset Maugham, for a searing example.

All this is true and important. But if we are seeking to get a handle on the problem of manipulation, definitions (1) through (8) capture a lot of the relevant territory, and the part of the territory that they capture is especially relevant to policy and law. If we keep definition (8) in mind, we can see an essential connection between the idea of manipulation and the idea of deception; we can even see the former as a lighter or softer version of the latter. Deceivers do not respect people's capacity for reflective and deliberative choice. With an act of deception, people almost inevitably[37] feel betrayed and outraged once they are informed of the truth. The same is true of manipulation. Once the full context is revealed, those who have been manipulated tend to feel betrayed or used. They ask: Why wasn't I allowed to decide for myself?

Illustrative Cases

Consider some cases that test the boundaries of the concept of manipulation.

1. *Relative risk information is (highly) manipulative.* Suppose that public officials try to persuade people to engage in certain behavior with the help of relative risk information: "If you do not do X, your chances of death from heart disease will triple!"[38] But suppose that for the relevant population, the chance of death

---

[37] They might be grateful, however, if the deception was genuinely undertaken in order to promote their interests.
[38] Wilkinson, *supra* note 13, at 347, uses this example.

from heart disease is very small – say, one in 100,000 – and that people are far more influenced by the idea of "tripling the risk" than they would be if they learned that if they do not do X, they could increase a 1/100,000 risk to a 3/100,000 risk. To say the least, that is a modest increase.

Or let's suppose the relevant statement comes from a doctor, who is trying to convince you to take a certain medication. The doctor says: "This medication can cut your annual risk of a stroke in half." Suppose that your background risk is 1 in 1,000, and that if you take the medication, the risk can be cut to 1 in 2,000. Suppose that the doctor is well aware that by phrasing the risk reduction as he did, he is increasing the chances that you will take the medication. Suppose that he is also aware that if he said that the medicine can reduce your risk from 1 in 1,000 to 1 in 2,000, two things might happen. First, you might be confused. Second, you might think, "One in 1,000 doesn't sound so bad, and one in 2,000 doesn't sound a lot different. No medicine, thank you!"

The relative risk frame is a bit terrifying. It is far more attention-grabbing than the absolute risk frame; a tripling of a risk sounds alarming, but if the increase is by merely 2/100,000, people might not be much concerned. It is certainly reasonable to take the choice of the relative risk frame (which suggests a large impact on health) as an effort to frighten people and thus to manipulate them (at least in a mild sense). It is plausibly a form of trickery that fits definition (1), and it certainly fits definition (2).

It is true that any description of a risk requires some choices; people who describe risks cannot avoid some kind of framing. But framing is not the same as manipulation. There is a good argument that this particular choice does not respect people's deliberative capacities; it might even be an effort to aim specifically at System 1. As we shall see, that conclusion does not mean that the use of the relative risk frame is necessarily out of bounds.[39] This is hardly the most egregious case of manipulation, and if it saves a number of lives

---

[39] *See* Craswell, Regulating Deceptive Advertising, *supra* note 24, at 552: "Advertisements are potentially dangerous 'products,' and advertisers should take reasonable steps to prevent consumers from being harmed by their products. But advertisers should not be faulted if any further changes would have made matters worse for consumers rather than better."

across a large population, it might be justified. But it can be counted as manipulative.

2. *Use of loss aversion may or may not be manipulative.* Suppose that public officials are alert to the power of loss aversion,[40] which means that people dislike the prospect of losses a lot more than they like the prospect of equivalent gains. "You will lose $1,000 annually if you do not use energy conservation strategies" might well be more effective than "you will gain $1,000 annually if you use energy conservation strategies." Suppose that officials use the "loss frame," so as to trigger people's concern about the risks associated with excessive energy consumption or obesity. They might deliberately choose to emphasize, in some kind of information campaign, how much people would lose from not using energy conservation techniques, rather than how much people would gain from using such techniques.[41] Is the use of loss aversion, with its potentially large effects, a form of manipulation?

The answer is not obvious, but there is a good argument that it is not, because people's deliberative capacities are being treated with respect. Even with a loss frame, people remain fully capable of assessing overall effects. They are not being tricked. But it must be acknowledged that the deliberate use of loss aversion might be an effort to trigger the negative feelings that are distinctly associated with losses.

It is a separate question whether the use of loss aversion raises serious ethical objections. Within the universe of arguably manipulative statements, those that enlist loss aversion hardly count as the most troublesome, and in the case under discussion, the government's objectives are laudable. If the use of loss aversion produces large gains (in terms of health or economic benefits), we would not have much ground for objection. But we can identify cases in which the use of loss aversion is self-interested, and in which the surrounding context makes it a genuine example of manipulation.[42]

---

[40] *See* Eyal Zamir, *Law, Psychology, and Morality: The Role of Loss Aversion* (2014).
[41] *See* Elliott Aronson, *The Social Animal* 124–5 (6th ed. 1996).
[42] *See* Lauren E. Willis, When Defaults Fail: Slippery Defaults, 80 *U Chicago Law Review* 1155 (2012).

Consider, for example, the efforts of banks, in the aftermath of a new regulation from the Federal Reserve Board, to enlist loss aversion to encourage customers to opt-in to costly overdraft protection programs by saying, "Don't lose your ATM and Debit Card Overdraft Protection" and "STAY PROTECTED with [ ] ATM and Debit Card Overdraft Coverage."[43] In such cases, there is an evident effort to trigger a degree of alarm, and hence it is reasonable to claim that customers are being manipulated, and to their detriment.

As a less egregious example from a consumer-facing company, consider the message that IndiGo, an Indian airline, presents to customers alongside the option to purchase an add-on travel assistance package (see Figure 1.1).

That is not the worst imaginable business practice, but it is fair to consider it to be a form of influence that does not respect people's capacity for reflective and deliberative choice.

3. *Use of social norms need not be manipulative.* Alert to the behavioral science on social influences,[44] a planner might consider the following approaches:
   a. Inform people that most people in their community *are engaging in undesirable behavior* (drug use, alcohol abuse, delinquent payment of taxes, environmentally harmful acts).
   b. Inform people that most people in their community *are engaging in desirable behavior.*
   c. Inform people that most people in their community *believe that people should engage in certain behavior.*

The first two approaches rely on "descriptive norms," that is, what people actually do.[45] The second approach relies on "injunctive norms," that is, what people think that people should do. As an empirical matter, it turns out that descriptive norms are ordinarily more powerful. If a change in behavior is what is sought, then it is best to emphasize that most people actually do the right

---

[43] *Ibid.* at 1192.
[44] For a summary, *see* Richard H. Thaler and Cass R. Sunstein, *Nudge: Improving Decisions about Health, Wealth, and Happiness* (2008).
[45] *See* Robert Cialdini, Crafting Normative Messages to Protect the Environment, 12 *Current Directions in Psychological Science* 105 (2003).

Figure 1.1 IndiGo Travel Assistance
Source: Deceptive Patterns, Hall of Shame, www.deceptive.design/hall-of-shame.

thing. But if most people do the wrong thing, it can be helpful to invoke injunctive norms.[46]

Suppose that public officials are keenly aware of these findings and use them. Are they engaging in manipulation? Without doing much violence to ordinary language, some people might think it reasonable to conclude that it is manipulative to choose the formulation that will have the largest impact. At least this is so if social influences work as they do because of their impact on the automatic system, and if they bypass deliberative processing.[47] But as an empirical matter, this is far from clear; information about what other people do, or what other people think, can be part of reflective deliberation, and hardly opposed to it. So long as the officials are

---

[46] *Ibid.*; Wesley Schultz et al., The Constructive, Destructive, and Reconstructive Power of Social Norms, 18 *Psychological Science* 429 (2007).
[47] For relevant (but not decisive) findings, *see* Caroline J. Charpentier et al., The Brain's Temporal Dynamics from a Collective Decision to Individual Action, 34 *Journal Neuroscience* 5816 (2014).

being truthful, it would strain the boundaries of the concept to accuse them of manipulation. When people are informed about what most people do, their powers of deliberation are being respected. No trickery is involved.

4. *Default rules may or may not be manipulative.* Default rules often stick, in part because of the force of inertia, in part because of the power of suggestion.[48] Suppose that a public official is aware of that fact and decides to reconsider a series of default rules in order to exploit the stickiness of defaults. Seeking to save money, she might decide in favor of a double-sided default for printers.[49] Seeking to reduce pollution, she might promote, or even require, a default rule in favor of green energy.[50] Seeking to increase savings, she might promote, or even require, automatic enrollment in retirement plans.[51]

Are these initiatives manipulative? Insofar as default rules carry an element of suggestion – a kind of informational signal – they are not. Such rules appeal to deliberative capacities and respect them to the extent that they convey information about what planners think people ought to be buying. The analysis is less straightforward insofar as default rules stick because of inertia: Without making a conscious choice, people end up enrolled in some kind of program or plan. In a sense, the official is exploiting System 1, which is prone to inertia and procrastination. The question is whether automatic enrollment fails to respect people's capacity for reflection and deliberation.

In answering that question, it is surely relevant that an opt-in default is likely to stick as well, and for the same reasons, which means that the question is whether *any* default rule counts

---

[48] *See* Eric Johnson and Daniel Goldstein, Decisions by Default, in *The Behavioral Foundations of Public Policy* 417 (Eldar Shafir ed. 2013); Cass R. Sunstein, *Choosing Not To Choose* (2015).
[49] *See* Johan Egebark and Mathias Ekström, Can Indifference Make the World Greener? (2013), available at www2.ne.su.se/paper/wp13_12.pdf.
[50] *See* Cass R. Sunstein and Lucia Reisch, Automatically Green: Behavioral Economics and Environmental Protection, 38 *Harvard Environmental Law Review* 127 (2014).
[51] Shlomo Benartzi and Richard H. Thaler, Behavioral Economics and the Retirement Savings Crisis, 339 *Science* 1152 (2013).

as a form of manipulation. The answer to that question is plain: Life cannot be navigated without default rules, and so long as the official is not hiding or suppressing anything and allows easy opt-out or opt-in, the choice of one or another should not be characterized as manipulative. Note that people do reject default rules that they genuinely dislike, so long as opt-out is easy – an empirical point in favor of the conclusion that such rules should not be counted as manipulative.[52]

Still, there is reason to worry that defaults can sometimes be manipulative.[53] Consider another case. A social media company defaults users into various terms with respect to privacy, newsfeed, reels, and community standards. Most of these can be changed, but they take effort. The platform's goal is to maximize engagement, which leads to profits. With respect to reels, for example, the platform will, by default, provide offerings that increase the likelihood that users will stay online. For some, those offerings will involve conspiracy theories; for others, they will involve make-up and clothes; for others, they will involve sexually explicit videos that suit their tastes. On reflection, many users would not choose these offerings, even if they will maximize engagement. Reflecting on what is best, users would choose something else. But by default, those are the offerings that they receive. We might well say that default rules can be a kind of trickery that do not respect people's capacity for reflective and deliberative choice.

Or consider a different case. If people rent a car online, they will, by default, receive a variety of terms. These include insurance of multiple kinds, including an agreement to pay a large amount if the car is not returned with a full tank of gas or a full charge of electricity, and "emergency road service" that turns out to be quite expensive. These default terms do not fit the circumstances of many renters. They cost too much. But if they are offered by default, consumers will tend to accept them. "From any user's perspective,

---

[52] See Zachary Brown et al., Testing the Effects of Defaults on the Thermostat Settings of OECD Employees, 39 Energy Economics 128 (2013); John Beshears et al., *The Limitations of Defaults* (Sept. 15, 2010) (unpublished manuscript), available at www.nber.org/programs/ag/rrc/NB10-02,%20Beshears,%20Choi,%20Laibson,%20Madrian.pdf.
[53] See Kalle Grill, Regulating Online Defaults, in *The Philosophy of Online Manipulation* 373 (Fleur Jongepier and Michael Klink eds. 2022).

it is best to be defaulted into an optimal situation. However, it is not reasonable to expect that others will arrange one's choice situations in such a way or even try to do so."[54]

Default terms of this kind might be counted as manipulative, certainly if they are not transparent and if choosers cannot readily change them. It makes sense to consider regulatory responses to provide information and to allow easy, one-click opt-out.

5. *Store design may be manipulative.* Suppose that a supermarket is engaged in self-conscious design, with a single goal: maximizing revenue. Suppose that it places certain products at the checkout counter, knowing that people will be especially willing to make impulse purchases. Those products include high-calorie, high-sugar foods and drinks. Suppose that the supermarket also places high-profit items in prominent places and at eye-level, hoping to encourage sales. Suppose that the supermarket has accumulated a lot of data on what works and what does not. It hopes to exploit attention and salience so as to increase sales. It knows exactly how to do that.

Is the supermarket engaged in manipulation? It is fair to say so. It is using various techniques in such a way as to reduce the likelihood of reflective and deliberative choice. Manipulation is involved. If evaluation of the (manipulative) store design is not at all obvious, it is for two reasons. First, no store can do without a design; some design is inevitable, and it will have an effect (see Chapter 7). Second, some designs are very much in the interest of shoppers. We can dispute whether a revenue-maximizing design falls in that category. Still, it might well be manipulative.

6. *Affect, attention, anchoring, and emotional contagion.* Much of modern advertising is directed at System 1, with attractive people, bold colors, and distinctive aesthetics. (Consider advertisements for Viagra.) Often the goal is to trigger a distinctive affect and more specifically to enlist the "affect heuristic," by which people evaluate goods and activities by reference to the affect they induce – which puts the question of manipulation in stark relief.[55]

[54] *Ibid.* at 381.
[55] *See* Paul Slovic ed., *The Feeling of Risk: New Perspectives on Risk Perception* 3–20 (2010).

The affect heuristic was originally identified by a remarkable finding: When asked to assess the risks and benefits associated with certain items, people tend to think that risky activities contain low benefits and that beneficial activities contain high risks.[56] In other words, people are likely to think that activities that seem dangerous do not carry benefits; it is rare that they will see an activity as both highly beneficial and quite dangerous, or as both benefit-free and danger-free. This is extremely odd. Why don't people think, more of the time, that some activity is both highly beneficial and highly risky? Why do they seem to make a kind of general, gestalt-type judgment, one that drives assessment of both risks and benefits? The answer appears to be "affect" comes first, and helps to direct judgments of both risk and benefit. Hence people are influenced by the affect heuristic, by which they have an emotional, all-things-considered reaction to certain processes and products. That heuristic operates as a mental shortcut for a more careful evaluation. The affect heuristic leaves a lot of room for manipulation. You can induce a positive or negative affect, and influence all kind of judgments, without respecting people's capacity for reflective and deliberative choice.

Much of website design is an effort to trigger attention and to put it in the right places.[57] Cell phone companies, restaurants, and clothing stores use music and colors in a way that is designed to influence people's affective reactions to their products. Doctors, friends, and family members (including spouses) sometimes do something quite similar. Is romance an exercise in manipulation? Some of the time, the answer is surely yes, though the question of whether people's deliberative capacities are being respected raises special challenges in that context.[58]

Acting as advocates, lawyers may be engaged in manipulation; that is part of their job, certainly in front of a jury. Suppose that a lawyer is aware of the power of "anchoring," which means that

---

[56] Paul Slovic et al., The Affect Heuristic, 177 *European Journal of Operational Research* 1333 (2007); Melissa Finucane et al., The Affect Heuristic in Judgments of Risks and Benefits, 13 *J of Behavioral Decision Making* 1 (2000).

[57] Steve Krug, *Don't Make Me Think Revisited: A Common Sense Approach to Web and Mobile Usability* (2014).

[58] I am aware of no detailed treatment of this question, but for relevant discussion, *see* Eric Cave, Unsavory Seduction and Manipulation, in *Manipulation: Theory and Practice* (Christian Coons and Michael Weber eds. 2014), at 176.

when people are asked to generate a number, any number put before them, even if it is arbitrary, may bias their judgments. Asking for damages for a personal injury, a lawyer might mention the annual revenue of a company (say, $1 billion) as a way of producing an anchor. That can be counted as a form of manipulation, because it does not respect people's deliberative capacities. If a salesperson uses an anchor to get people to pay a lot for a new motor vehicle, manipulation is also involved, and for the same reasons.

The same can be said about some imaginable practices in medical care. Suppose that doctors want patients to choose particular options, and enlist behaviorally informed techniques to manipulate them to do so. An example would be to use the availability heuristic, by which people assess risks by asking whether examples come readily to mind. If a doctor uses certain examples ("I had a patient who died when ..."), we might have a case of manipulation, at least if the examples are being used to bypass or subvert deliberative judgments.

Or return to certain uses of social media – as we saw, for example, in 2012, when Facebook attempted to affect (manipulate) the emotions of hundreds of thousands of people though the display of positive or negative stories to see how they affected their moods.[59] Numerous practices on social media platforms, however familiar, can be counted as manipulative in the relevant sense.

A Checklist

Anne Barnhill has devoted a lot of time and effort to defining manipulation, but she is aware that efforts at definition are challenging, and that it may not be possible to come up with a definition that commands a consensus.[60] She urges that instead of worrying about whether a practice fits the definition, we might ask questions that might illuminate why some people see it as manipulative. Here are some of her questions, slightly revised:

- Is the influence covert or hidden?
- Does the influence target, or play on, psychological weaknesses or vulnerabilities? These could be psychological weaknesses or

[59] See Kramer et al., *supra* note 1.   [60] See Barnhill, *supra* note 4.

vulnerabilities in the specific targeted individual or of people in general.
- Does the influence subvert people's self-control?
- Does the influence fail to engage people in deliberation or reflection? If so, is deliberation or reflection called for in the context?
- Does the influence cause people to have emotional reactions? Are these appropriate or inappropriate emotional reactions, given the context?
- Does the influence undermine rationality or practical reasoning in some way?

A checklist of this kind is helpful, because the questions it asks may be easier to handle than the question whether some statement or action counts as manipulative. Many cases of dark patterns, understood as deceptive or manipulative practice online, can be handled by reference to such questions, even if we struggle to decide whether those cases involve manipulation. We will get there in short order.

2 EVALUATING MANIPULATION

When is manipulation wrong? Why is it wrong?

Some forms of manipulation produce a smile and a nod. If your partner asks you to do a little work around the house, and adds with a seductive look, "I promise to make it worth your while," you might feel manipulated, but you might not much mind. If a political advertisement features upbeat, stirring music for the candidate, and ugly, jarring music for the opponent, you might think, "That's what politics is all about, I guess." If an advertisement for a new car features attractive people going to a fancy party, you might think, "I see just what they're doing there."

But sometimes manipulation produces a much more negative reaction. People feel outraged or humiliated. They might think that manipulation is a form of theft. Someone is stealing something from them. In fact that is a large part of the picture.

R-E-S-P-E-C-T

The most obvious problem with manipulation is that it can insult both autonomy and dignity. An act of manipulation does not treat people with respect. From the standpoint of autonomy, the problem is that manipulation can deprive people of agency; it is a close cousin to coercion. If people are manipulated into buying a product, they might even feel coerced.

From the standpoint of dignity, one problem is that manipulation can be humiliating. Healthy adults, not suffering from a lack of capacity, should not be tricked; they should be treated as fully capable of making their own decisions. Their authority over their own lives should not be undermined by approaches that treat them as children or as puppets. As Marcia Baron puts it, "The virtuous person tries to reason with the other, not cajole or trick him into acting differently .... being manipulative is a vice because of its arrogance and presumption, and because the manipulative person is too quick to resort to ruses ...."[1]

Suppose, for example, that someone thinks, "I want all my friends to do certain things, and I know a number of strategies to get them to do those things. I have read a great deal of psychology and behavioral science, including the best work on social influence, and my project is to use what I know to manipulate my friends."[2] Such a person would not be respecting her friends' autonomy. She would be using them as her instruments. Indeed, her actions would be inconsistent with the nature of friendship itself, which entails a relationship that is not strictly or mostly instrumental.

Now turn to the case of government. Suppose that public officials – say, in a president's office – similarly learn a great deal about how to influence people, and suppose that they decide to use what they learn to achieve certain policy goals. Suppose that some of the relevant instruments attempt to subvert or bypass deliberation. We need to know the details – What, exactly, are they doing? – but it could well be fair to say that manipulation is involved, and that public officials are not sufficiently respecting their citizens' autonomy. Again we need to know the details, but it could also be fair to

---

[1] *See* Marcia Baron, Manipulativeness, 77 *Proceedings and Addresses of the American Philosophical Association* 37 (2003), and more broadly this suggestion: "By contrast, the person who has the virtue corresponding to manipulativeness – a virtue for which we do not, I believe, have a name – knows when it is appropriate to try to bring about a change in another's conduct and does this for the right reasons, for the right ends, and only where it is warranted (and worth the risks) and only using acceptable means. The virtuous person tries to reason with the other, not cajole or trick him into acting differently ... being manipulative is a vice because of its arrogance and presumption, and because the manipulative person is too quick to resort to ruses ...." *Ibid.* at 48, 50.

[2] A classic source here is Robert Cialdini, *Influence* (2006); another classic, far less academic but highly informative, is Dale Carnegie, *How to Win Friends and Influence People* (1998). Both books can be seen as offering a great deal of advice about successful manipulation.

say that such officials are not treating citizens with respect; they might be using them as instruments or as puppets for their own ends (or perhaps the public-spirited ends that they favor).

We should be able to see, in this light, that *role* greatly matters to the assessment of manipulation. Suppose that Jones is trying to obtain a job. It is hardly unacceptable for Jones to attempt to get prospective employers to like him, and if Jones learns about behavioral science and how to influence people, it would hardly be illegitimate for him to take advantage of what he learns. To be sure, there are ethical limits on what Jones can do, and even for someone seeking a job, the most egregious forms of manipulation would cross the line. But in interactions or relationships that are instrumental, and that are so understood, some of the ethical constraints are weakened or at least different.

In an advertising campaign, everyone knows the nature of the interaction. Manipulation is the coin of the realm. The purpose of advertisements is to sell products, and while we can find purely factual presentations, many advertisements do not appeal to reflection or deliberation at all. They try to create certain moods and associations. Something similar can be said about some aspects of political campaigns. The relationship between a campaign and voters has an instrumental character: Campaigns want votes, and everyone understands that. In the process, both advertisements and speeches will have manipulative features. To be sure, it would be extravagant to say that, in such cases, people have consented to manipulation in all imaginable forms. Here too, lines can be crossed. (Prechecked boxes can cross those lines.) But it is important that people are aware of the distinctive nature of the relevant enterprises.

Other roles are accompanied by different norms, and manipulation might not fit with, or might even violate, those norms. When governments deal with their citizens, they face radically different norms from those that apply in campaigns. At least this is so in free and democratic societies, in which it is understood that the public is ultimately sovereign. To be sure, public officials are hardly forbidden from framing options in a way that casts those they prefer in the most favorable light. But as the manipulative characteristics of their actions become more extreme, the scope for legitimate objection becomes greater.

Welfare

Suppose that we are welfarists, which means that we believe that what matters is how people's lives are going.[3] We want to know whether people are sad or happy, calm or tense, relaxed or frightened, distressed or joyful. Suppose too that we care about violations of autonomy and dignity insofar as such violations affect people's subjective experiences (for example, by making them feel angry or humiliated). If so, how should we think about manipulation?

It should be clear that *there is no taboo on the practice.* Welfarists are willing to accept lies and deception if they will make people's lives go better, and the same is true of manipulation, which might promote people's welfare. If a doctor manipulates a patient into taking medicine that will save her life, we might have no ground for objection. Still, there is a distinctive welfarist objection to manipulation, which takes the following form. Much of the time, at least, choosers know what is in their best interests (at least if they are adults, and if they do not suffer from a problem of capacity[4]). They know that they like tennis more than bowling, or dogs more than cats, or Taylor Swift more than Drake, or romantic comedies more than horror movies. They have unique access to their situations, their constraints, and their tastes. If they are manipulated, they are deprived of the (full) ability to make choices on their own, simply because they are not given a fair or adequate chance to weigh all variables. If someone wants to help people to make better choices, his obligation is to inform them, so that they can themselves engage in such weighing.

---

[3] I am bracketing here various questions about how welfarism is best understood. It is possible to have a conception of welfare that includes consideration of autonomy and dignity. See Amartya Sen, *Development as Freedom* (2000); Martha Nussbaum, *Creating Capabilities* (2011); Amartya Sen, Utilitarianism and Welfarism, 76 *Journal of Philosophy* 463 (1979). For instructive discussion, *see* Matthew Adler, *Welfare and Fair Distribution* (2011).

[4] A child, or a person suffering from some form of dementia, has a weaker objection to manipulation. Parents manipulate young children all the time, partly to promote their welfare. Caretakers manipulate people who are suffering from dementia. These practices are largely taken for granted, but we could imagine situations in which they would raise serious ethical questions. Even if the relevant manipulation is in the interest of those who are being manipulated, the interests in autonomy and dignity impose constraints even here.

The problem with the manipulator is that he lacks relevant knowledge – about the chooser's situation, tastes, and values. Lacking that knowledge, he nonetheless subverts the process by which choosers make their own decisions about what is best for them. Things are even worse if the manipulator is focused on his own interests rather than on those of choosers. It is in this sense that a self-interested manipulator can be said to be stealing from people – both limiting their agency and moving their resources in the preferred direction.

For these reasons, the welfarist objection to paternalism is rooted in the same concerns that underlie John Stuart Mill's Harm Principle. In Mill's view, the problem with outsiders, including government officials, is that they lack the necessary information. Mill insists that the individual "is the person most interested in his own well-being,"[5] and the "ordinary man or woman has means of knowledge immeasurably surpassing those that can be possessed by any one else." When society seeks to overrule the individual's judgment, it does so on the basis of "general presumptions," and these "may be altogether wrong, and even if right, are as likely as not to be misapplied to individual cases." These points apply to those engaged in manipulation no less than to those engaged in coercion.

Notwithstanding these points, it should be clear that from the welfarist standpoint, there should be no ban on manipulation.[6] Everything depends on whether manipulation improves people's welfare. A manipulator might not respect people's capacity for reflective and deliberative choice, but nonetheless might improve their welfare.

To see the point, imagine a benign, all-knowing, welfare-promoting manipulator – a kind of idealized parent – who is concerned only with the welfare of those who are being

---

[5] John Stuart Mill, *On Liberty* 8 (Kathy Casey ed. 2002) (1859).
[6] Note that the question here is whether manipulation increases or decreases welfare; it is not whether the law, or some regulator, should ban manipulation. The latter question raises issues about institutional competence and decision costs. It also requires attention to the effect of manipulation on large populations with heterogeneous understandings. In response to an advertising campaign, for example, some people might be manipulated (in the sense that System 1 is essentially all that is affected) while others are not (because the campaign triggers a significant amount of deliberation).

manipulated, who has all the knowledge he needs, and who simply does not make mistakes. By hypothesis, the welfare-promoting manipulator should be celebrated on welfarist grounds.[7] The major qualification is that if people know that they are being manipulated, and do not like it, there will be a welfare loss, and that loss will have to be counted in the overall assessment. The simple point is that if people hate manipulators, manipulation is less likely to be supportable on welfare grounds (unless it is hidden, which raises problems of its own[8]).

But put that point to one side. The main problem with the thought experiment is that manipulators are unlikely to be either benign or all-knowing. Usually, they have their own agendas, and the fact that they engage in manipulation attests to that fact. If they are genuinely concerned about the welfare of the chooser, why not try to persuade them? Why cross the line to manipulation? To be sure, the manipulator might be able to answer this question if, for example, time is of the essence, or if the chooser lacks capacity (because, for example, he is a child or very ill). Or suppose that graphic health warnings, manipulating people, save numerous lives; suppose too that numerous lives cannot be saved with a merely factual presentation unaccompanied by graphic health warnings. On welfarist grounds, a great deal might be said on behalf of graphic health warnings.[9]

The example shows that from the standpoint of welfare, everything depends on the context; the fact that manipulation is involved does not *necessarily* impeach the manipulator's welfare calculus. But in many situations, suspicion about manipulators' goals is perfectly justified. To this point it must be added that even when those goals are admirable, manipulators may not know enough to justify their actions. Consider Friedrich Hayek's remarkable suggestion that "the awareness of our irremediable ignorance of most of what is known to somebody [who is a chooser] is *the chief*

---

[7] Compare the vigorous defense of coercive paternalism in Sarah Conly, *Against Autonomy* (2012).
[8] Hidden manipulation is risky, because it might be disclosed, and people will not be happy to learn that it has been hidden.
[9] Christine Jolls, Product Warnings, Debiasing, and Free Speech: The Case of Tobacco Regulation, 169 *J Institutional and Theoretical Economics* 53 (2013).

basis of the argument for liberty."[10] I will return to this point, and the question of regulation, in due course.

Consent

Suppose that people consent to manipulation.[11] An alcoholic might tell his wife: "I am trying so hard to quit. Please use whatever techniques you can think of to help me. Manipulation is very much on the table. I welcome it!" Or suppose that the overwhelming majority of smokers tell their government: "I really want to stop! If you can find a way to help me to overcome my addiction, I would be grateful." T. M. Wilkinson notes that it is too crude to say that manipulation infringes upon autonomy, because "manipulation could be consented to. If it were consented to, in the right kind of way, then the manipulation would at least be consistent with autonomy and might count as enhancing it."[12]

The conclusion has a great deal of force. The tale of Ulysses and the Sirens is instructive here, whether Ulysses was requesting coercion, manipulation, or something else.[13] In fact he requested coercion:

> She [Circe] said we must avoid the voices of the otherworldly Sirens; steer past their flowering meadow. And she says that I alone should hear their singing. Bind me, to keep me upright at the mast, wound round with rope. If I beseech you and command to set me free, you must increase my bonds and chain even tighter.

Nor is there an obvious objection, in the case of consent, from the standpoint of welfare. The chooser has decided that he will be better off if he is manipulated. If we see his choice as

---

[10] *See* Frederick Hayek, The Market and Other Orders, in *The Collected Works of F. A. Hayek* 384 (Bruce Caldwell ed. 2013) (emphasis added).
[11] On one view, the concept of manipulation presupposes a lack of consent. *See* Robert Goodin, *Manipulatory Politics* 9 (1980) (discussing the idea of "unknown interference"). But the examples given in the text suggest that manipulation can be a product of consent and even invitation.
[12] T. M. Wilkinson, Nudging and Manipulation, 61 *Political Studies* 341, 342 (2013), at 345.
[13] *See* Jon Elster, *Ulysses and the Sirens* (1983).

presumptively promoting his welfare, we should respect it, even if what he chose is manipulation.

In the easiest cases, consent is explicit. In harder cases, it is only implicit, in the sense that the manipulator infers it from the circumstances or believes, with good reason, that the chooser would consent if asked. If the inference is less than reliable, the consent justification is correspondingly weakened. If the belief is reasonable but potentially wrong, it would make sense to insist on obtaining explicit consent in order to avoid the risk of error. It is important to see that consensual manipulation is an unusual case; those who need help do not ordinarily ask, "Please manipulate me." But such cases certainly do exist, at least when people face serious problems of self-control.

Transparency

The idea of manipulation is sometimes taken to imply a lack of transparency, as if something important is being hidden or not being disclosed.[14] If a manipulator is acting as a puppeteer, he might be failing to reveal his own role; that can be an important feature of manipulation. With respect to manipulation, however, it is not entirely clear what transparency even means.

Sometimes manipulation itself *consists* in a lack of transparency about a relevant feature of a situation; that is the very manipulation involved. (A parent tells a small child: If you are very good, Santa Claus will bring you a toy giraffe.) Once the relevant feature is revealed, the manipulation is gone. But the manipulative character of some acts does not consist in their hidden quality. (Recall the use of relative risk reduction.) Some acts can be both manipulative and fully revealed to those who are being manipulated.[15] A graphic health warning, for example, is perfectly transparent (and if it is required by regulation, it might even be preceded by a period for public comment). Subliminal advertising could be preceded by an explicit warning: "This movie contains subliminal advertising."

[14] *See* Goodin, *supra* note 11, at 7–12.
[15] For relevant findings, *see* Gidon Felsen et al., Decisional Enhancement and Autonomy: Public Attitudes toward Overt and Covert Nudges, 8 *Judgment and Decision Making* 203 (2012).

In the pivotal scene in *The Wizard of Oz*, the Wizard says, "Pay no attention to the man behind the curtain." The man behind the curtain is, of course, a mere human being who is masquerading as the great Wizard – and who is both claiming far more authority than he deserves and designing social situations in a way that hides features that, if revealed, would greatly alter people's judgments and choices. Or consider a terrific but less celebrated movie, *The Truman Show*, in which the life course of Truman, the movie's hero-protagonist, is affected by multiple decisions from a master manipulator, who conceals the facts that Truman is the unwitting star of a television show and that his friends and acquaintances consist of actors. Covertness and hiding are forms of trickery, and they are common features of manipulation. Whenever people who are imposing influence conceal their own role, it seems reasonable to object. A lack of transparency offends both autonomy and dignity.

From the standpoint of welfare, we might ask why, exactly, someone has failed to be upfront with the chooser, who ought to be able to make his own decisions, armed with relevant information. As before, however, the analysis of welfare is more complex, for we could imagine cases in which transparency is not necessary and may in fact be a problem. Suppose that someone suffers from a serious self-control problem and that his life is in danger (from, say, alcohol or drug addiction). Suppose too that a manipulator has come across a life-saving strategy and that transparency would render the manipulation less effective. By hypothesis, welfarist considerations argue against transparency. Points of this kind have the strongest intuitive force when applied to people who lack capacity (young children, the mentally ill), but we can imagine contexts in which adults with full capacity would benefit from being manipulated.[16]

There might also be a welfarist justification for hidden manipulation in other extreme circumstances – as, for example, when people are trying to stop a kidnapping or to save a kidnapping

---

[16] Conly, *supra* note 7, 149–72, offers a series of cases in which, on her view, coercion is justified, among other things on welfare grounds. If manipulation passed the relevant tests (involving cost-benefit analysis and cost-effectiveness, *ibid.* at 150–2), it would be justified on similar grounds. Conly herself offers cautionary notes about manipulation, pointing to its uneasy relationship with autonomy. *Ibid.* at 30–1.

victim. If the goal is to stop a wrongdoer, or someone who threatens to do real harm, it may be perfectly acceptable or even obligatory to manipulate them and to hide that fact. They have forfeited their right to be treated with respect, and their welfare, as choosers, is not a matter of much concern.

In standard cases, however, this argument will be unavailable. It follows that most of the time, manipulation should not be hidden or covert, even when it is justified; return to the case of graphic health warnings (which may or may not qualify as manipulative). Transparency is a necessary condition. Note, however, that it is not sufficient. Subliminal advertising would not become acceptable merely because people were informed about it. If a movie chain announced that its previews would be filled with subliminal advertisements, people could fairly object.

As an objectionable example of a lack of transparency, consider musician and media personality Eric July's online membership offering (see Figure 2.1). Customers are offered a subscription for $99.99 monthly, but the fact that it is a "monthly" subscription is displayed in text that is the same color as the web page's background. The fact that customers are opting into a recurring subscription is not so transparent, and the low level of transparency suggests that we are dealing with a case of manipulation.

Figure 2.1 Eric July online membership
Source: Deceptive Patterns, Hall of Shame, www.deceptive.design/hall-of-shame.

Figure 2.2 Papa John's cash back
Source: Deceptive Patterns, Hall of Shame, www.deceptive.design/hall-of-shame.

Issues of transparency arise in varying degrees. Consider the cash back offer from Papa John's shown in Figure 2.2.

The offer does state that by accepting £16.87 cash back, the customer is agreeing to a subscription that costs £15/month. Still, this condition is not fully transparent. What is the user most likely to notice? The subscription and its price are in objectionably small print.

Democratic Authorization

What if manipulation is democratically authorized? Suppose that a national legislature expressly votes for it, perhaps in order to improve public health (as, for example, by discouraging smoking or unhealthy eating), or perhaps to promote other goals (such as voting or patriotism). In relatively benign cases, involving little or no manipulation, a legislature might support an educational campaign that is designed to reduce illnesses and deaths and that enlists a series of behaviorally informed strategies to accomplish its goals.

It should be clear that democratic authorization ought not by itself to dissolve otherwise convincing objections to manipulation. The most obvious problems arise if the national legislature has illegitimate ends (say, the inculcation of racial prejudice or self-entrenchment of some kind). But the familiar objections – involving autonomy, dignity, and welfare – apply even if the ends are legitimate. If a national legislature authorizes subliminal advertising, it remains fully possible to object on grounds of both autonomy and dignity. An objection from the standpoint of welfare is also possible: Why did the democratic process authorize manipulation, rather than some other kind of communication? Would that other kind be more likely to increase welfare?

To be sure, we could understand democratic authorization as a form of majority or collective consent; people might welcome a little manipulation (or possibly a lot). But why should a majority be allowed to consent to manipulation of everyone? And there are evident risks in authorizing public officials to pursue this line of argument. The objection to manipulation comes from individuals who do not want to be manipulated; the fact that a majority wants to manipulate them is no defense.

But in certain contexts, the argument on behalf of at least a modest degree of manipulation might not be entirely implausible, and it is strengthened if the democratic process has supported it. Imagine, for example, a public education campaign that is designed to reduce the risks associated with texting while driving, or an effort to combat the use of dangerous drugs or to convince people to stay in school. Many such campaigns are vivid and have an emotional component; they can be understood as efforts to combat self-control problems and to focus people on the long term. They may or may not respect people's capacity for reflective and deliberative choice. They ought to do so, but on imaginable assumptions about their beneficial effects, perhaps we should not fuss about them too much.

If government is manipulating people – perhaps through emotionally evocative appeals – it might be responding to the fact that people have already been manipulated and to their detriment. In the context of cigarettes, for example, it is plausible to say that previous manipulations – including advertising and social norms – have influenced people to become smokers. If this is so, perhaps we can say that public officials are permitted to meet fire with fire. But it is reasonable to insist that two wrongs do not make a right – and that if the government seeks to lead people to quit, it must treat them as adults, and appeal to their deliberative capacities.

Recall that there are degrees of manipulation, and there is a large difference between a lie and an effort to frame an alternative in an appealing, unappealing, or ugly light. In ordinary life, we would not be likely to accuse our friends or loved ones of manipulation if they characterized one approach as favored by most members of our peer group, or if they emphasized the losses that might accompany an alternative that they abhor, or if they accompanied a description of one option with a grave look and a frown. We have seen that these are at most mild forms of manipulation, if they count at all, and it is important to see that mild forms might well be acceptable and benign (and a bit fun) if they promote the interests of those people at whom they are aimed.

3 THE RIGHT NOT TO BE MANIPULATED

In 1890, Louis Brandeis and Samuel Warren proposed a new right: the right to privacy.[1] They urged that modern society creates a host of new threats to people's right to be let alone. They pointed to the importance of seclusion – of being able to maintain private spaces. Noting that the right to privacy had multiple faces, they argued that free societies should recognize a broad and general right. As they put it: "Political, social, and economic changes entail the recognition of new rights.... [N]ow the right to life has come to mean the right to enjoy life, – the right to be let alone."

Their argument was and remains immensely influential. It spoke to the anxieties of the age. Even more, it speaks to the anxieties of the current era. The threats to privacy are not the same, of course. But the general idea of a right to privacy has helped to orient discussion and understanding for well over a century.

Recall this statement from the White House in 2024: "Americans should not be subject to confusing, manipulative, or deceptive practices online."[2] Should there be a right not to be manipulated? Ought that right to be seen as something comparable

---

[1] Samuel D. Warren and Louis D. Brandeis, The Right to Privacy, 4 *Harvard Law Review* 193 (1890), 194.

[2] *See* Biden-Harris Administration Launches New Effort to Crack Down on Everyday Headaches and Hassles That Waste Americans' Time and Money (Aug. 12, 2024), www.whitehouse.gov/briefing-room/statements-releases/2024/08/12/fact-sheet-biden-harris-administration-launches-new-effort-to-crack-down-on-everyday-headaches-and-hassles-that-waste-americans-time-and-money/.

to the right to privacy in 1890? I think so, but (as they say) it's complicated.

Consider in this light some instructive experiments conducted by Jamie Luguri and Lior Strahilewitz.[3] Luguri and Strahilewitz were interested in dark patterns and their effects on consumers. In one of their experiments, they tested the effect of making it easy for people to choose a costly identity theft protection program. In the control condition, people could choose that program if they wanted – but they would have to choose it by clicking on a button. In one of the treatment conditions, it was simpler for users to accept the program, because it was the default choice; they did not have to click on any button. It was harder to decline it, because they had to click on "other options" before seeing how to do that. Accepting the program was also labeled as "recommended." This was a pretty mild dark pattern, but it produced a big shift in favor of the program – from 11.3 percent acceptance in the control condition to 25.8 percent in the treatment condition. Notably, the mildly manipulative intervention had a much larger effect on less educated consumers than on well-educated consumers.

Luguri and Strahilewitz also tested the effect of various other dark patterns designed to promote the costly program. They found that if information about the price was hidden in small, gray print, more people would choose it. They also found that if "accept" was the default choice, and if people had to do more work to decline it, acceptance rates jumped. They found too that a trick question, making it difficult for consumers to understand what they were choosing or declining, significantly increased acceptance rates. Notably, increasing the cost of the program had no effect on people's susceptibility to online manipulation. This, then, is powerful evidence that manipulative practices can have a big effect on choosers.

Speaking of Rights

Most legal systems recognize a right not to be deceived. If we understand deception as intentionally leading people to have false beliefs, we can see that at least in the commercial domain,

---

[3] See Jamie Luguri and Lior Strahilewitz, Shining a Light on Dark Patterns, 13 *J Legal Analysis* 43 (2021).

deception is generally against the law. If I market a pill as "a guaranteed cure for baldness," and the pill does nothing at all to cure baldness, I have probably acted unlawfully. If I sell you a new kind of aspirin and claim that it prevents cancer when it does nothing of the kind, I can probably be punished. It is true that deception is not always policed. If I deceive you into believing that climate change is not real, nothing bad will happen to me. One reason is that freedom of speech requires some breathing room for errors, and even for deliberate falsehoods. We will get to that.

We should now be able to agree that a more-or-less identifiable category of actions counts as manipulation; that those actions do not respect people's capacity for agency; that those actions are often unacceptable for that reason; that those actions often lead people in directions that make their lives worse, perhaps because the manipulator is evil or self-serving, perhaps because the manipulator is at an epistemic disadvantage compared to the chooser. Manipulators try to seduce choosers to do as they wish, and they often succeed.

In these circumstances, there is a strong argument for a right not to be manipulated. We should see that right as rooted in a principle of decisional autonomy, supported for different reasons by Kantians and welfarists, and operating against both private and public institutions. Companies should not manipulate their customers. Governments should not manipulate their citizens.

I have pointed to cases in which the right not to be manipulated might be defeasible. A terrorist, or someone engaged in domestic abuse, forfeits that right. But moral rights of all kinds are not absolute. The right to free speech is not absolute, and the same is true for the right to freedom of religion. A right not to be manipulated is especially important in the modern era, when the capacity to manipulate people, especially online, is far greater than ever before.

Markets and Information

In this light, we should be very glad to have a social norm against manipulation, and we might want to fortify it, perhaps to protect against self-serving marketers or politicians.[4]

---

[4] *See* Robert E. Goodin, *Manipulatory Politics* (1980).

Friedrich Hayek, the greatest critic of socialist-style planning, explored the relationship between free markets and knowledge. Some of Hayek's most important contributions to social thought are captured in his great (and short) 1945 essay, "The Use of Knowledge in Society."[5] In that essay, Hayek claimed that the great advantage of prices is that they aggregate both the information and the tastes of numerous people, incorporating far more material than could possibly be assembled by any central planner, group, or board. Hayek emphasized the unshared nature of information – the "dispersed bits of incomplete and frequently contradictory knowledge which all the separate individuals possess." That knowledge certainly includes facts about products, but it also includes preferences and tastes, and all of these are taken into account by a well-functioning market. Hayek stressed above all the "very important but unorganized knowledge which cannot possibly be called scientific in the sense of general rules: the knowledge of the particular circumstances of time and place."

For Hayek, the key economic question is how to incorporate that unorganized and dispersed knowledge. No particular person or group can possibly solve that problem. Central planners cannot have access to all of the knowledge held by diverse people. Taken as a whole, the knowledge held by those people is far greater than that held by even the wisest and most well-chosen group or experts. Hayek's central point is that the best solution often comes from the price system. His claim is that in a system in which knowledge of relevant facts is dispersed among many people, prices act as an astonishingly concise and accurate coordinating and signaling device. They incorporate that dispersed knowledge, and in a sense also publicize it, because the price itself operates as a signal to all.

Even better, the price system has a wonderfully automatic quality, particularly in its ability to respond quickly to changes. If fresh information shows that a product – a television, a car, a cell phone, a watch – does not always work, people's demand for it will

---

[5] Frederick Hayek, The Use of Knowledge in Society, 35 *American Economic Review* 519–30 (1945). Superb treatments of Hayek's thought include Peter Boettke, *F. A. Hayek: Economics, Political Economy and Social Philosophy* (2018); Bruce Caldwell, *Hayek's Challenge: An Intellectual Biography of F. A. Hayek* (2004).

rapidly fall, and so too the price. And when a commodity suddenly becomes scarcer, its users must respond to that fact. In Hayek's account, the market works remarkably well as a whole, not because any participant can see all its features, but because the relevant information is communicated to everyone through prices.

Hence Hayek claims that it "is more than a metaphor to describe the price system as a kind of machinery for registering changes, or a system of telecommunications which enables individual producers to watch merely the movement of a few pointers."[6] Hayek describes this process as a "marvel," and adds that he has chosen that word on purpose so as "to shock the reader out of the complacency with which we often take the working of the mechanism for granted." On Hayek's account, the price system is an extraordinary device for capturing collective intelligence, in part because it collects what everyone knows, and in part because it imposes the right incentives.

For present purposes, here is the key point: All this depends on a system that is relatively free from deception and manipulation. If consumers are subject to both of these, the marvel will not be so marvelous. And even if deception and manipulation are occasional rather than widespread, a lot of people might be hurt. Perhaps market pressures will prevent them, or at least reduce their incidence. Under optimistic assumptions, that is right. But we can easily imagine situations in which market pressures promote deception and manipulation, rather than the opposite. If manipulation in particular is profitable, then companies that do not manipulate will be at a competitive disadvantage. That appears to be true in many markets.

Vagueness and Overbreadth

Even so, we might be tempted to think that manipulation falls in a category of actions properly promoted or discouraged by social norms, but generally unaccompanied by law or regulation. On the positive side, we might speak of kindness, considerateness,[7]

---

[6] Hayek, The Use of Knowledge, *supra* note 5, at 526.
[7] *See* Edna Ullmann-Margalit, *Normal Rationality: Decisions and Social Orders* (Avishai Margalit and Cass R. Sunstein eds. 2017).

civility, grace, and generosity. No law requires these things. On the negative side, we might speak of unkindness, incivility, gracelessness, and meanness. No law punishes unkindness, inconsiderateness, gracelessness, and meanness. But why is that?

The first reason is *vagueness*. Many norms, including those that protect moral rights, are directed against conduct that is not, and cannot be, defined with sufficient precision for law. This problem raises two concerns. The first is that people will not have fair notice about what they can and cannot do; they will not be able to plan. The second is that enforcement authorities will have undue discretion to pick and choose. People might find that they are in a lottery: They might be singled out for no obvious reason. Or they might find that they are in a nightmare: They might be singled out because of their skin color or their gender.

Vagueness is a real problem for a right not to be manipulated. We have seen that in ordinary language, and even as elaborated by the most careful philosophers, manipulation cannot easily be the foundation for criminal law and regulation. I like my definitions, but I cannot say that definition (1) in Chapter 1, or definition (2), should be part of the law of the land.

The second reason is *overbreadth*. Many categories of bad conduct include a large assortment of actions, some of which are not so bad as to warrant punishment, and some of which might not be bad at all in the circumstances. People also have a right to be bad, so long as they are not all that bad. That is one reason that unkindness, incivility, and inconsiderateness are not unlawful. As we have seen, that point certainly holds for manipulation. A world without manipulation would be no fun. Who wants never to be seduced?

We might think that terms like "fraud" and "assault" have similar problems, and that thought is not entirely wrong. Still, longstanding traditions are available to specify and to concretize such terms, greatly weakening concerns about vagueness and overbreadth. The same cannot be said of manipulation.

You might wonder about the difference between vagueness and overbreadth. Here is a way of understanding it. Suppose that a law forbids any speech that is not protected by the First Amendment to the United States Constitution. That law would not be overbroad. By definition, it does not permit any speech that the First Amendment does not protect! Still, such a law would be unacceptably vague. The reason is that First Amendment law is exceptionally complicated and in many ways unclear; it would not give people fair notice.

Targeting Egregious Manipulation

Still, there is a great deal that can be done, starting by focusing on the worst cases – the most egregious practices, defined as those that are hardest to justify and that are most likely to impose real harm. We have seen that in some such cases, manipulative behavior is a form of theft, and when that is so, it should be forbidden for that reason. (Compare lying, which is not forbidden, with libel, which is.) We do best by focusing on specific practices of manipulative behavior – those that are plainly harmful and very hard to defend on any ground.

A great deal of attention is now being paid to an assortment of online practices going under the name of dark patterns[8] or deceptive patterns. The term, meant to capture deception and manipulation, includes the following:

1. **Scarcity** ("only 15 left!").
2. **Social proof** ("Taylor Swift loves it!" or "Join millions of happy customers!").
3. **Activity message** (information on the level of activity on a site, such as views or visits).
4. **Countdown timer** ("only an hour left!").
5. **Drip pricing** (it is $200 – but there are add-on prices at checkout).
6. **Hidden costs** (costs are disclosed late, or are obscured).
7. **Hidden information/terms** (for example, automatic monthly payments, balloon payments, privacy sacrificed).
8. **Hidden subscription** (a recurring fee, not clearly disclosed).
9. **Sneak into basket** (adding products to shopping cart without obtaining people's consent).
10. **Obstruction** (making it difficult to reject or see certain terms).

---

[8] *See* Harry Brignull, *Deceptive Patterns* (2023); Mather et al., *Dark Patterns at Scale* (2019).

11. **Roach motel** (an easy click to subscribe, a phone call or more to unsubscribe).
12. **Forced action** (requiring people to say whether they want to decline to enroll in some expensive program before completing purchase).
13. **Confirmshaming** ("I don't care about my privacy" or "I don't care about protecting my health").
14. **Nagging/bombarding** ("buy soon or you lose your chance," stated repeatedly, perhaps by text messages).

Some of these practices are far worse than others. Take, for example, a practice by the Donald Trump campaign in March 2020, reflective of (7) in the list above. People who donated to the campaign were directed to an online form which, amidst a lot of other fine print, contained a prefilled check mark reading, "Make this a monthly recurring donation."[9] In June of the same year, the campaign used a similar strategy, called "the money bomb," to default people into making an additional donation for Trump's birthday.[10] In September, the campaign changed "a monthly recurring donation," with that small check mark, into "a weekly recurring donation."[11]

As the campaign continued, the "weekly recurring donation" box was made less conspicuous and moved beneath other text, thus combining (6) and (7) in the list above.[12] These strategies worked. They created a surge in donations, including a large number of unintended payments, which, in many cases, exceeded credit card limits, requiring people to pay overdraft fees to their banks, and leading people to cancel their cards to avoid recurring payments. By one calculation, the use of "dark defaults," as they have been called, increased revenue by $42 million. Remarkably, donors showed little learning.[13]

---

[9] Shane Goldmacher, How Trump Steered Supporters into Unwitting Donations, *New York Times* (updated Aug. 7, 2021), www.nytimes.com/2021/04/03/us/politics/trump-donations.html; *see also* Nathaniel Posner et al., Dark Defaults: How Choice Architecture Steers Campaign Donations (Oct. 29, 2022) (unpublished manuscript), https://papers.ssrn.com/sol3/papers.cfm?abstract_id=4258478.

[10] Goldmacher, *supra* note 9. [11] Ibid. [12] Ibid.

[13] *See* Posner et al., *supra* note 9.

When do prechecked boxes, a form of (7) in the list above, count as manipulation, and as a form of theft? To answer those questions, we need to answer two further questions: (1) Are prechecked boxes entirely transparent and visible? (2) Are they in the interest of all or most who are affected by them? If the answer to both questions is "yes," we do not have manipulation, and we do not have a problem. If the answer to both questions is "no," we have manipulation, and we have a serious problem. Indeed, we should find manipulation if the answer to the first question is "no," even if the answer to the second question is "yes." The reason is that people are not put in a position to make a deliberative choice. If the answer to the first question is "yes" but the answer to the second question is "no," we do not have manipulation (even if we have another kind of problem).

It is important to see that by themselves, prechecked boxes are hardly manipulative, and they might be a terrific idea. A cellphone or a laptop has the equivalent of prechecked boxes, including default settings, and they are a blessing. If people are told explicitly that a company that sells an online service (such as Netflix, Apple, or Amazon) will automatically renew their subscription, it is not at all clear that the law should intervene. To be sure, it matters whether most people, given the choice, would favor automatic renewal.

The most serious problems arise when people *are not given clarity that they are committing themselves to certain terms* – and when the relevant terms are highly unlikely to be what people would have chosen if they had known about the choice. As a general rule, there should be a prohibition on billing people in accordance with terms to which they did not actively consent, certainly in cases in which they would not do that if they had been asked.[14] Here is one of the darkest of dark patterns, and it is a form of theft. It should be forbidden. Drip pricing is also a form of manipulation and hence theft; it too should be forbidden.

Consider image Figure 3.1. The term of the subscription is far from clear, and that must be by design.

---

[14] I am painting with a broad brush. On some of the complexities, *see* Margaret Jane Radin, *Boilerplate: The Fine Print, Vanishing Rights, and the Rule of Law* (2012).

Figure 3.1 Adobe subscription billing
Source: Deceptive Patterns, Hall of Shame, www.deceptive.design/hall-of-shame.

In Figure 3.1, the user is enrolling in an annual subscription, billed monthly.[15] If you cannot find this information in the image, it is not your fault. The only time interval displayed is the monthly payment interval. It is not at all clear that the user is also signing up for a one-year term.

To protect against manipulation, the underlying principle should be one of decisional autonomy, which means that hidden fees and costs belong in a prohibited category. Regulators should take firm aim at those fees and costs. In a representative action in 2012, the Department of Transportation required U.S. air carriers and online travel agents to alter their web interfaces to incorporate all ticket taxes in upfront, advertised fares. The goal is to allow consumers to make informed choices. Evidence suggests that this behaviorally informed intervention, designed to overcome shrouded prices, has been highly effective and thus saved consumers a great deal of money.[16]

---

[15] Deceptive Patterns, Hall of Shame, www.deceptive.design/hall-of-shame.
[16] *See* Sebastien Bradley and Naomi E. Feldman, Hidden Baggage: Behavioral Responses to Changes in Airline Ticket Tax Disclosure, 12 *American Economic J: Economic Policy* 58 (2020).

In 2024, the Department of Transportation issued a final rule that requires airlines and airfare ticketing agents to disclose charges for checked baggage, carry-on baggage, changes, and cancelations upfront as customers are considering their purchases.[17] Also in 2024, the Federal Communications Commission required Internet service providers to display standardized "broadband nutrition labels."[18] The standardized labels are meant to enable customers to compare providers' offerings like-for-like, and include standardized price details, data allowances, and broadband speeds. In the same year, the Consumer Financial Protection Bureau (CFPB) proposed a rule that would limit overdraft fees charged by financial institutions with more than $10 billion in assets to an amount "in line with their costs or in accordance with an established benchmark."[19] The CFPB's proposed rule included a set of benchmark figures, with the highest set at $14.[20]

A New Right, Established

In 2024, the White House announced an all-of-government attack on dark patterns of diverse kinds, under what it called a "Time Is Money" initiative.[21] With an explicit emphasis on manipulation, the initiative can easily be seen as an incarnation of a right not to be manipulated. The government announced:

---

[17] Biden-Harris Administration Announces Final Rule to Protect Consumers from Surprise Airline Junk Fees, U.S. Department of Transportation (Apr. 24, 2024), www.transportation.gov/briefing-room/biden-harris-administration-announces-final-rule-protect-consumers-surprise-airline.

[18] *See* Brian Fung, FCC Rolls Out Mandatory "Nutrition Labels" for Internet Providers' Plans, CNN (Apr. 10, 2024), https://edition.cnn.com/2024/04/10/tech/fcc-mandatory-nutrition-labels-internet-providers/index.html; Broadband Consumer Labels, Federal Communications Commission (May 7, 2024), www.fcc.gov/broadbandlabels; Consumer Fact Sheet: Broadband Consumer Label Required For Most Internet Service Providers, Federal Communications Commission, https://docs.fcc.gov/public/attachments/DOC-401799A1.pdf.

[19] CFPB Proposes Rule to Close Bank Overdraft Loophole that Costs Americans Billions Each Year in Junk Fees, Consumer Financial Protection Bureau (Jan. 17, 2024), www.consumerfinance.gov/about-us/newsroom/cfpb-proposes-rule-to-close-bank-overdraft-loophole-that-costs-americans-billions-each-year-in-junk-fees/.

[20] *Ibid.*   [21] *See supra* note 2.

Americans should not be subject to confusing, manipulative, or deceptive practices online.

- *If you want to understand what you must do to obtain a good or service, the requirements should be clear and transparent.*
- *You should not be subject to hidden fees or to requirements that are obscured through confusing language and small print.*

Let us pause over that. True, a mere announcement cannot create a legally enforceable right, but the core of a right not to be manipulated is contained in those words.

Among other things, and consistent with the analysis here, the initiative attacks covert or hidden terms and fees. It also targets what it describes as "doom loops," by which people are "sent through a maze of menu options and automated recordings, wasting their time and failing to get the support they need." In response, the government proposes to "require companies under its jurisdiction to let customers talk to a human by pressing a single button."[22]

Taking aim at manipulation, the government notes that companies "often trick consumers into paying for subscriptions – on everything from gym memberships to newspapers to cosmetics – that they no longer want or didn't sign up for in the first place." In response, it endorses a rule that "would require companies to make it as easy to cancel a subscription or service as it was to sign up for one." A governing principle is clear: "It should be as easy to obtain rebates and refunds as it was to purchase, with no needlessly cumbersome paperwork."

Here is another principle: "If you want to talk to a human, you should be able to talk to a human at convenient times and without interminable waits." And here is another: "You should not be subject to hidden fees or to requirements that are obscured through confusing language and small print."[23]

---

[22] *See* www.whitehouse.gov/briefing-room/statements-releases/2024/08/12/fact-sheet-biden-harris-administration-launches-new-effort-to-crack-down-on-everyday-headaches-and-hassles-that-waste-americans-time-and-money/.
[23] *Ibid.*

By contrast, some dark patterns, even if they are plausibly regarded as manipulative, are not easily seen as a form of theft, and as a general rule, they should not be forbidden by law. Consider three examples:

1. Suppose that people are repeatedly requested to do something: "Wouldn't you like to buy this book?" Frequent requests, also known as *nagging*, are annoying, and we cannot rule out the possibility that some people will be worn down. There is a "pressure account" of manipulation, and under that account, some kinds of nagging can be manipulative.[24] But a reminder is not the worst thing in the world, and if people eventually agree to buy the product or to accept an offer, it might be because they decide, on reflection, that it is in their interest to do so. A frequent request can overcome limited attention and inertia, and we might want to assume that many or most people end up making a reasonable choice. To be sure, some cases of nagging, whether or not they count as manipulative, might be so egregious, and so annoying, that they should be outlawed.

2. Suppose that consumers are told (truthfully) that supplies are limited, or suppose that some kind of countdown timer is used to promote a sense of urgency ("only two hours left!"). It is not so easy to see these practices, also known as *scarcity*, as theft, and it is hard to justify legal intervention. But if the relevant claims are false – if supplies are not relevantly lifted or if there are plenty of hours left – then we have a case of fraud.

3. Uses of *social proof* might be manipulative in some cases, but it is hard to see why they should be forbidden, at least if they are truthful. If some celebrity really does like a product, there is nothing wrong with informing people of that fact. And if there are numerous satisfied customers, it is not improper to disclose their satisfaction. To be sure, false uses of social proof would not merely be manipulative; they would be deceptive.

In thinking about whether to proscribe manipulation, we do best to target and to build on the most egregious cases, and to draw up categories for regulation with close reference to them. Recall that

---

[24] *See* Robert Noggle, Pressure, Trickery, and a Unified Account of Manipulation, 57 American Philosophical Quarterly 245 (2020).

lies, as such, are not a violation of the law; it is libel that is a violation of the law, and the same is true for perjury and false advertising. Where lies are prohibited, it is because they do serious damage; in some cases, they are a form of theft. They undermine or eliminate people's ability to make their own decisions. They take something from some people for the benefit of others. In some cases, manipulative practices have the same character. That is when, and why, the law should target them.

In the context of consumer financial products, various forms of manipulation are a widespread problem. Indeed, manipulation can be seen as a defining motivation for some regulatory initiatives. The Dodd-Frank Wall Street Reform and Consumer Protection Act states that the CFPB should ensure that "markets for consumer financial products and services are fair, transparent, and competitive."[25] It calls for attention not only to "unfair and deceptive" acts and practices but also to "abusive" ones, which can be seen as a reference to the worst forms of manipulation. In monitoring the relevant markets, the CFPB must consider the "understanding by consumers of the risks of a type of consumer financial product or service"[26] – a phrase that can easily be taken to reflect a concern about manipulation.

Implementing these requirements, the CFPB adopted as its slogan, "know before you owe," and its various efforts to ensure informed choices can be understood as an attack on manipulation as I have understood it here.[27] In consumer markets, of course, one problem is complexity, which can defeat understanding, and which can be manipulative in its own right; return to definitions (1) and (8) in Chapter 1. Different practices also fall in the general category of manipulation; consider "teaser rates" and various inducements that fall short of deceit, but that emphatically prey on people's weaknesses, and that do not respect people's capacity for reflective and deliberative choice.

A short, simple credit card agreement, of the sort provided by the CFPB, can be seen as a direct response to the risk of

---

[25] 12 U.S.C. 5511. [26] 12 U.S.C. 5512.
[27] *See* Know Before You Owe: Credit cards, Consumer Financial Protection Bureau, www.consumerfinance.gov/data-research/credit-card-data/know-you-owe-credit-cards/.

manipulation[28] – and as an effort to ensure that System 2 is firmly in charge. Proposals to ban or restrict teaser rates can be understood in similar terms.[29] In cases of this kind, there is ample room for considering the problem of manipulation in deciding how best to regulate financial products. It is important to see that in such cases, government is regulating commercial practices, not advertising, and that its real concern is with practices that do not respect reflective and deliberation choice on the part of consumers. The CFPB's initiatives can easily be taken as efforts to combat manipulation.

Regulating Speech

Under established doctrine, government can regulate threats;[30] it can also regulate false or misleading commercial speech.[31] May it also regulate manipulation? It is clear that government can compel certain kinds of speech.[32] May it compel speech that is arguably manipulative?

As a testing case, consider the efforts of the Food and Drug Administration (FDA) to require cigarette packages to contain graphic health warnings. In 2011, the FDA finalized a rule mandating a series of such warnings. Consider, for example, Figure 3.2.

Are such warnings unacceptably manipulative? A federal court of appeals invalidated the requirement on the First Amendment grounds, concluding that the FDA lacked sufficient evidence to justify the compelled speech.[33] In so ruling, the court did not emphasize the arguably manipulative nature of the graphic warnings. But the lower court opinion did exactly that.[34]

---

[28] *Ibid.*
[29] Oren Bar-Gill and Ryan Bubb, Credit Card Pricing: The Card Act and Beyond, 97 *Cornell Law Review* 967 (2012).
[30] *Watts v. United States*, 394 U.S. 705 (1969).
[31] *Virginia State Pharmacy Board v. Virginia Citizens Consumer Council*, 425 U.S. 748 (1976).
[32] *Johanns v. Livestock Marketing Association*, 544 U.S. 550 (2005); Bianca Nunes, The Future of Government-Mandated Health Warnings, 163 *U Pa Law Review* 177 (2014).
[33] *R.J. Reynolds Tobacco Co. v. FDA*, 696 F.3d 1205 (D.C. Cir. 2012).
[34] See *RJ Reynolds Tobacco Co. v. FDA*, 823 F. Supp.2d 36 (2011).

Figure 3.2 FDA warning labels, 2011
Source: *New Graphic Warning Labels Designed to Reduce the Deadly Effects of Smoking*, Obama White House Archives (Jun. 21, 2011), https://obamawhitehouse.archives.gov/blog/2011/06/21/new-graphic-warning-labels-designed-reduce-deadly-effects-smoking-0.

The court found it relevant that "the Rule's graphic-image requirements are *not* the type of purely factual and uncontroversial disclosures that are" subject to less critical judicial scrutiny.[35] It added, plausibly, that "it is abundantly clear from viewing these images that the emotional response they were crafted to induce is calculated to provoke the viewer to quit, or never to start, smoking: an objective wholly apart from disseminating purely factual and uncontroversial information."[36] The court concluded that when the government compels speech that does not involve the "purely factual and uncontroversial," it has to meet a higher burden of justification. This, then, is a challenge to government efforts to compel a kind of manipulative speech from private companies.

The central idea here lacks clear support in Supreme Court decisions, but it has some appeal: The First Amendment imposes particular barriers to government efforts to require speech that does not respect deliberative or reflective capacities, but that engages and attempts to activate System 1. On this view, there is no absolute rule against compelling manipulative speech of that kind (so long as it is not false or deceptive), but if government is engaging in such compulsion, it must have a strong justification for doing so.

---

[35] *Ibid.* at 45 (emphasis added). [36] *Ibid.*

This analysis raises an assortment of issues. Do the graphic warnings count as manipulative? They are certainly designed to create a visceral response (and they do exactly that). But the question is whether they respect people's capacity for reflective and deliberative choice. There is an empirical question here: What, exactly, do people understand after they see the warnings? Suppose that for a large part of the population, understanding is actually improved. If so, there is a good argument that manipulation is not involved. But suppose that understanding is not improved. Can the warnings nonetheless be justified?

We could imagine two such justifications. The first is welfarist: Graphic health warnings will save a significant number of lives, and purely factual information will have a far weaker effect. If this is so, then the graphic health warnings do have a sufficient justification. The second is rooted in autonomy: Smokers, and prospective smokers, do not sufficiently appreciate the health risks of smoking, and graphic warnings can promote a kind of "debiasing" that statistical information fails to provide.[37] To this point, it might be added that government regulation is hardly being imposed on a blank slate. Recall that efforts to promote smoking involve a high degree of manipulation – portraying happy, healthy, attractive smokers – and perhaps the government can legitimately respond. In light of the number of lives at risk and the underlying evidence, these kinds of justifications do seem sufficient in the particular context of smoking.

The FDA produced a new series of graphic warnings for cigarette packaging in 2019, including the images shown in Figure 3.3, which are a bit milder than those reprinted in Figure 3.2.

The FDA stated that strong evidence suggested that warnings of this kind would inform consumers of the relevant risks – and thus produce more educated choices.[38] The court of appeals upheld the regulation requiring these warnings, stating that they were "both factual and uncontroversial."[39] The FDA's eminently

---

[37] Ibid.
[38] See the account at www.federalregister.gov/documents/2020/03/18/2020-05223/tobacco-products-required-warnings-for-cigarette-packages-and-advertisements.
[39] See R.J Reynolds v. FDA (2024), available at www.ca5.uscourts.gov/opinions/pub/23/23-40076-CV0.pdf.

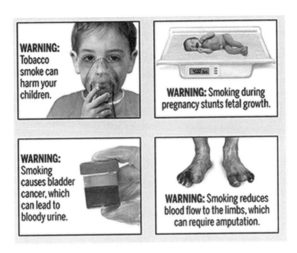

Figure 3.3 FDA warning labels, 2019
Source: Food and Drug Administration. See the various documents at www.fda.gov/tobacco-products/labeling-and-warning-statements-tobacco-products/cigarette-labeling-and-health-warning-requirements.

sensible requirements, and the court's eminently sensible decision, demonstrate that graphic warnings need not be unacceptably manipulative; they can respect people's capacity for reflective and deliberative choice.

Part II
APPLICATIONS

4 DEEPFAKES: MANIPULATED BY TECHNOLOGY

Can you tell which of the images shown in Figure 4.1 are real, and which are deepfakes? (Answer: They are both deepfakes.)

As you almost certainly know, deepfakes are products of techniques, based on artificial intelligence, for creating apparently real images or videos, in which people might be shown doing or saying something that they never did or said.[1] It is easy to produce them. If you feed a few images into a site, you can generate plenty of deepfakes, showing the relevant person looking thin, fat, ugly, beautiful, elegant, or naked. If an image of a person can be found, the technology is now available to create a deepfake making it look as if the person is a professional athlete or a drug addict, hates black people, despises his country, engages in shoplifting, or dances wildly to terrible songs – anything at all. Deepfake pornography is now pervasive.[2] Deepfakes can easily be used to discredit your neighbor, your enemy, or your least favorite candidate for public office. They can also be used to put people in an exceptionally favorable light.

Deepfakes are often described as "manipulated media," meaning not that they are manipulative, but that some form of technological manipulation is at work. Still, the problem of manipulation, as I am understanding it here, is central to deepfakes. They manipulate people. If you display a famous popular singer using

---

[1] Marc Jonathan Blitz, Lies, Line Drawing, and (Deep) Fake News, 71 *Okla Law Review* 59, 61 (2018).
[2] Danielle Keats Citron, Sexual Privacy, 128 *Yale Law Journal* 1870, 1921–2 (2019).

Figure 4.1 Deepfakes
Sources: 26 deepfakes that will freak you out, CNET (2020), www.cnet.com/pictures/26-deepfakes-that-will-freak-you-out/; Stuart Thompson, A.I. Is Getting Better Fast. Can You Tell What's Real Now?, *The New York Times* (2024), www.nytimes.com/interactive/2024/06/24/technology/ai-deepfake-facebook-midjourney-quiz.html.

cocaine, you will trick System 1 (and maybe System 2 as well). Seeing is believing, as they say. If you see a realistic depiction of something that never happened, you will have to work a bit to dislodge the sense, in some part of your mind, that in fact, it actually did happen. Deepfakes lead people to believe something without respecting their deliberative capacities.

Of course it is also fair and right to describe deepfakes as a form of deception. They are manipulative, but they are also a lie.

Liars

Should political and legal systems permit lies? What kind of lie? We might approach this question through the lens of U.S. constitutional law, which offers an intriguing perspective.

It was not until 2012 that the U.S. Supreme Court made it clear that false statements and lies, as such, fall within the ambit of the First Amendment, which protects "the freedom of speech." In *United States v. Alvarez*,[3] a badly divided Court held that the First Amendment prohibited a criminal prosecution of a person who falsely claimed that he was a recipient of the Congressional Medal of Honor.

The case involved Xavier Alvarez, an inveterate liar who falsely claimed, among other things, that he had been a Vietnam veteran, a police officer, married to an actress from Mexico, and a professional hockey player for the Detroit Red Wings. But he got into trouble with the law when serving as a board member of the Three Valley Water District Board, a governmental entity with headquarters in Claremont, California. He said this:

> I'm a retired marine of 25 years. I retired in the year 2001. Back in 1987, I was awarded the Congressional Medal of Honor. I got wounded many times by the same guy.[4]

None of that was true! One part of it was also illegal. His claim to have received the Medal of Honor violated the Stolen Valor Act, which makes it a crime to make that particular lie. Nonetheless, the Supreme Court ruled that the lie was protected by the First Amendment.

In explaining why this grotesque and intentional falsehood was protected, the plurality spoke grandly:

> Permitting the government to decree this speech to be a criminal offense, whether shouted from the rooftops or made in a barely audible whisper, would endorse government authority to compile a list of subjects about which false statements are punishable. That governmental power has no clear limiting principle. Our constitutional tradition

[3] 567 U.S. 709 (2012). [4] *Ibid.*

stands against the idea that we need Oceania's Ministry of Truth. Were this law to be sustained, there could be an endless list of subjects the National Government or the States could single out.[5]

Among other things, the Justices who agreed with the result emphasized that punishing false speech would deter free debate. They added that less restrictive alternatives, including "counterspeech," could promote the state's legitimate interests (such as not diluting the effect of actual receipt of the Congressional Medal of Honor). But how much would counterspeech help? Would it help with deepfakes? That is a really good question; we will get to it in due course.

We should agree that government ought not to be given unbounded "authority to compile a list of subjects about which false statements are punishable." If Congress made it a crime to make a false statement about climate change or about evolution, or about football or baseball, or about American, German, or Russian history, it would be acting in violation of the First Amendment. A Ministry of Truth would indeed run afoul of the First Amendment. One reason is that there is a difference between a mere falsehood and a lie; the speaker's state of mind matters. (The plurality elided this difference; Alvarez lied!) Another reason is that for many questions, it is right to say the government must rely on counterspeech, in the form of some kind of rebuttal, and not on censorship or punishment.

Manipulation and Doctored Videos

Let us understand "doctored videos" as products of techniques by which a real video is altered to make it seem as if people are doing or saying something other than what they did, or differently from how they did it.[6] A doctored video might show people

---

[5] *Ibid.* at 723 (citing George Orwell, *Nineteen Eighty-Four* (1949) (Centennial ed. 2003)).

[6] *See, e.g.*, BBC News, Fake Obama Created Using AI Video Tool, YouTube (July 19, 2017), www.youtube.com/watch?v=AmUC4m6w1wo [https://perma.cc/89DT-Y4C6]; Fortune Magazine, What Is a Deepfake? Video Examples with Nicolas Cage, Jennifer Lawrence, Obama Show Troubling Trend, YouTube (Mar. 11, 2019),

supporting a cause that they abhor, committing a crime, showing disloyalty to their country, acting inappropriately when they did nothing of the kind, or being inebriated or otherwise impaired. In some cases, doctored videos are quite credible, in the sense that viewers do not believe that they have been doctored. They might turn out to be harmful, misleading, manipulative, or libelous.[7] I will be mostly speaking here of deepfakes, but the analysis applies to doctored videos more broadly.

For orientation – and for a sense of what is here and bound to get much worse – consider some hypothetical cases:

- Jane Jones is a high school teacher. A deepfake shows her in a romantic situation with a student.
- Philip Cross is a candidate for public office. A deepfake shows him endorsing Hitler and the Holocaust.
- John Simons is eighty years old. A deepfake shows him taking an "energy pill" and then competing fiercely and well in a pickup basketball game.
- A deepfake shows the Beatles playing Taylor Swift songs.
- A deepfake shows the Mona Lisa speaking like a teenager.
- A deepfake shows a Labrador Retriever dancing like Michael Jackson.
- A deepfake shows the Attorney General of the United States looking drunk and disoriented.

The decision of the U.S. Supreme Court in *Alvarez* might well be taken to suggest that deepfakes should not and cannot be regulated simply because they are deepfakes. They are essentially

---

www.youtube.com/watch?v=-yQxsIWO2ic [https://perma.cc/WW9F-JZ9F]; Bernhard Warner, Deepfake Video of Mark Zuckerberg Goes Viral on Eve of House A.I. Hearing, Fortune (June 12, 2019, 12:31 PM), https://fortune.com/2019/06/12/deepfake-mark-zuckerberg [https://perma.cc/52PM-2DGE].

[7] *Corp. Training Unlimited, Inc. v. Nat'l Broad. Co.*, 868 F. Supp. 501, 507 (E.D.N.Y. 1994) (explaining that when scrutinizing "audio and video portions of a television program," courts should be cognizant of "the possibility that a transcript which appears relatively mild on its face may actually be ... highly toxic," and that "a clever amalgamation of half-truths and opinion-like statements, adorned with orchestrated images and dramatic audio accompaniment, can be devastating when packaged in the powerful television medium").

falsehoods, and to that extent, they are protected unless they cause harm.[8] Do they cause any?

For the people who are used in deepfakes, the harm takes the form of reputational injury. A deepfake can be favorable or innocuous, but it can also be akin to or a form of defamation; it can hold people up to ridicule or contempt in their communities. Actually it can be devastating. People can be portrayed in the most horrible way imaginable, whether we are speaking of foolishness, criminality, corruption, or evil (or something related to sex). If a deepfake is defamatory – if its propositional content amounts to a libel – it can be regulated in many nations, including the United States. Apart from injuring the person who is depicted, it can injure the community by, for example, discrediting a candidate for public office and thus distorting the democratic process. We should underline that point. When one of us is defamed, a lot of us might be hurt.

But deepfakes, as such, need not be libelous at all. As we have seen, they might be positive; they might make people look impressive or wonderful. They might be a lie, or manipulative, for that reason. For example, they might show a politician or an actor, or a professor who is interested in the topic of manipulation, playing tennis or golf at a professional level. They might show a public figure (say, a candidate for public office) doing something admirable or heroic. That too can be harmful. A deepfake might fail to respect people's capacity for reflective and deliberative choice. It is obviously a form of trickery.

If people do not believe that a deepfake is real, of course, there should be no harm. If a rock group from the 1960s (two members of whom are dead) is seen playing songs by a contemporary musician, we are dealing with something like whimsy, humor, or

---

[8] In *Alvarez*, Justice Breyer noted that "few statutes, if any, simply prohibit without limitation the telling of a lie, even a lie about one particular matter. Instead, in virtually all these instances limitations of context, requirements of proof of injury, and the like, narrow the statute to a subset of lies where specific harm is more likely to occur." 567 U.S. 709, 736 (2012) (Breyer, J., concurring). He continued by explaining that "the limitations help to make certain that the statute does not allow its threat of liability or criminal punishment to roam at large, discouraging or forbidding the telling of the lie in contexts where harm is unlikely or the need for the prohibition is small." *Ibid.*

satire – all of which should be protected by the First Amendment.[9] The risk of harm arises if and when people think that what they are seeing actually happened. If people are falsely shown in a romantic situation or endorsing a political position that they abhor, they may in fact be harmed.

In this light, consider the following proposition:

> The government can and should regulate or ban deepfakes, consistent with protection of freedom of speech, if (1) it is not reasonably obvious or explicitly and prominently disclosed that they are deepfakes, and (2) they would create serious reputational harm.

Note that (2) is meant to build on the existing law of libel.[10]

Here is a possible response, inspired by the prevailing opinion in *Alvarez*: The best answer to a deepfake is counterspeech and disclosure, not censorship. That is true for both private institutions and public officials. The idea of "reputational harm" is too vague.

A social media provider, such as YouTube or Meta, might conclude that platform users should be notified that deepfakes are deepfakes. It might reject the view that doctored videos should be taken down. It might conclude that users should be able to see those videos so long as they receive the information they need to put the videos into perspective. As the plurality put it in *Alvarez*: "The remedy for speech that is false is speech that is true. This is the ordinary course in a free society."[11] Some social media platforms have sometimes adopted an approach of this kind, requiring labels for manipulated media (and also taking down tweets if they are "likely to cause harm").[12]

---

[9] *Hustler Magazine, Inc. v. Falwell*, 485 U.S. 46, 54 (1988).
[10] Even if deepfakes did not threaten to harm their subjects, they could nonetheless cause harm. Consider, for example, a deepfake that portrays a political candidate as doing something heroic when he did nothing of the kind.
[11] *Alvarez*, 567 U.S. at 727.
[12] Building rules in public: Our Approach to Synthetic & Manipulated Media, Twitter Blog (Feb. 4, 2020), https://blog.twitter.com/en_us/topics/company/2020/new-approach-to-synthetic-and-manipulated-media.html. The blog post elaborates:

> Some specific harms we consider include:
> - Threats to the physical safety of a person or group
> - Risk of mass violence or widespread civil unrest

As a matter of constitutional law, something similar might be said about what governments may do. Perhaps they should be required to choose the approach that is maximally protective of speech. In *Alvarez*, for example, the plurality explained: "The Government has not shown, and cannot show, why counterspeech would not suffice to achieve its interest. The facts of this case indicate that the dynamics of free speech, of counterspeech, of refutation, can overcome the lie."[13] It added: "There is, however, at least one less speech-restrictive means by which the Government could likely protect the integrity of the military awards system. A Government-created database could list Congressional Medal of Honor winners. Were a database accessible through the Internet, it would be easy to verify and expose false claims."[14]

But it would be exceedingly difficult to defend the view that this is a sufficient response to deepfakes. Suppose that someone is portrayed as doing something that she never did or as endorsing a position that she despises. If so, an accessible database would be most unlikely to undo the damage. Perhaps the speech-protective approach would be clear disclosure, informing people, before they see the video, that it is fake. Under *Alvarez*, there should be no constitutional barrier to that kind of control on deepfakes, at least on a sufficient showing of harm – and the same analysis applies to doctored videos.

What is that sufficient showing? Libel is a good answer, but it is not the only one. If people get the impression that someone did something that they did not do, there can be harm for that very reason. This is so whenever a deepfake makes people believe that someone did something that they did not do.

A Property Right in One's Person

Suppose that we are focused on manipulation and deception. Should government go beyond disclosure? Should it be

- Threats to the privacy or ability of a person or group to freely express themselves or participate in civic events, such as: stalking or unwanted and obsessive attention; targeted content that includes tropes, epithets, or material that aims to silence someone; voter suppression or intimidation.

[13] *Alvarez*, 567 U.S. at 726.   [14] *Ibid.* at 729.

permitted to do that? More aggressive controls might take the form of fines and an order to cease and desist, enforced perhaps by an independent commission. Or they could operate via a tort-like approach, operating through a civil cause of action, building on libel law, and creating a kind of property right in one's person.

It is tempting to respond that, in an important sense, deepfakes and doctored videos are nothing new. They are equivalent to false statements of fact. If a deepfake depicts the Attorney General looking drunk and disoriented, perhaps it is not so different, or any different, from this apparently credible statement: "I saw the Attorney General looking drunk and disoriented." The propositional content of deepfakes, in the form of such statements, is not regulated or banned (unless there is an independent ground – for example, they might be defamatory or obscene). Why should deepfakes themselves be treated differently?

A reasonable answer is that deepfakes (and doctored videos) have a unique kind of authenticity; they are more credible than merely verbal representations. In a sense, they are self-authenticating. That is why they are manipulative as well as deceptive. The human mind does not easily dismiss them, and if it does, there is some part of it that remains convinced. Consider here "the truth bias."[15] The truth bias is the basic human tendency to believe what we are told. We tend to assume that others are telling the truth because they usually are. Suppose, for example, that you are in a new town and you ask strangers for directions. It will probably not cross your mind that they are trying to get you lost.

If you see a deepfake of a drunk Attorney General, you will have a hard time getting the image out of your mind. The image manipulates you. For these reasons, it is plausible to say that deepfakes (and doctored videos) are properly the objects of regulatory attention even if statements that embody their propositional content are not. And as we have seen, some false statements of fact, seriously harmful to the political process, may be regulable even if they are not defamatory.

For private institutions, an aggressive approach would be quite reasonable. For governments, a prominent disclosure mandate

---

[15] I. Skurnik et al., How Warnings about False Claims Become Recommendations, 31 *J Consumer Research* 713 (2005).

should be upheld for deepfakes and doctored videos. And in cases of palpable harm, they might want to go further.

What To Do

These conclusions have strong implications for television networks and for social media platforms such as Meta, YouTube, and X. Imaginable restrictions could protect, separately or at once, democratic processes and individual lives. In 2019, Facebook responded to considerations of this general kind with an announcement that it was banning deepfakes.[16] That was an important step in the right direction. But was it enough?

As Facebook then pointed out, media can be manipulated for benign reasons, such as making video sharper and audio clearer. Some forms of manipulation are clearly meant as jokes, satires, parodies, or political statements – as, for example, when a rock star or a politician is depicted as a giant or as having superpowers. That is not a basis for regulation by government or by Facebook. Under its 2019 policy, Facebook said that it will remove "misleading manipulative media" only if two conditions are met:

- "It has been edited or synthesized – beyond adjustments for clarity or quality – in ways that aren't apparent to an average person and would likely mislead someone into thinking that a subject of the video said words that they did not actually say."[17]
- "It is the product of artificial intelligence or machine learning that merges, replaces or superimposes content onto a video, making it appear to be authentic."[18]

In a sense, the first condition is close to what I have suggested here. The average person must, by hypothesis, be reasonable. There is no requirement of serious harm (and perhaps there should be no such requirement insofar as we are dealing with regulation by a private institution, not a government). The two conditions were meant to be tailored to Facebook's concern: use of new or emerging

---

[16] Monika Bickert, Enforcing Against Manipulated Media, Facebook (Jan. 6, 2020), https://about.fb.com/news/2020/01/enforcing-against-manipulated-media [https://perma.cc/A4SV-878X].
[17] Ibid.   [18] Ibid.

technologies to mislead the average person into thinking that someone said something that they never said. Facebook's 2019 announcement also made it clear that even if a video is not removed under the new policy, other safeguards might be triggered.[19] If, for example, a video contains graphic violence or nudity, it will be taken down.

That approach should be seen as significant progress, and in the future other social media platforms would do well to consider it.

YouTube's approach has been both more and less aggressive; at one point, it flatly forbade "[v]ideo content that has been technically manipulated (beyond clips taken out of context) to fabricate events where there is a serious risk of egregious harm."[20] Note that YouTube imposed a requirement of egregious harm, as Facebook did not. The term is lamentably vague, but it is clearly meant to allow manipulated media that is funny or satirical, or that is meant as some kind of social commentary.

But under Facebook's 2019 approach, two problems remained. The first was that even if a deepfake was involved, the policy did not apply if the deepfake depicted deeds rather than words. (Recall the first condition, suggesting that the deepfake must depict a subject of the video saying, "words that they did not actually say.") Suppose that artificial intelligence is used to show a political candidate working with terrorists, beating up a small child, or using heroin. Nothing in the 2019 policy addressed those depictions. That was a serious gap. Deepfakes should be banned on social media platforms if they depict actions that would otherwise fall within the 2019 prohibition, even if no one is shown to have said anything.

The second problem is that the prohibition was limited to products of artificial intelligence or machine learning. Why did or would that restriction make sense? Suppose that videos are altered in other ways – for example, by slowing them down so as to make

---

[19] Ibid.; see also Guy Rosen, Helping to Protect the 2020 US Elections, Facebook (Oct. 21, 2019), https://about.fb.com/news/2019/10/update-on-election-integrity-efforts [https://perma.cc/Q6DV-YA4Q] (announcing additional safeguards to reduce the impact of viral misinformation on U.S. elections).

[20] Spam, Deceptive Practices, & Scams Policies, YouTube Help, https://support.google.com/youtube/answer/2801973?hl=en.

someone appear drunk or drugged, as in the case of an infamous doctored video of then-Speaker of the House Nancy Pelosi. Or suppose that a series of videos, directed against a candidate for governor, is produced not with artificial intelligence or machine learning, but nonetheless in such a way as to run afoul of the first condition; that is, they have been edited or synthesized so as to make the average person think that the candidate said words that she did not actually say. What matters is not the particular technology used to deceive people, but whether unacceptable deception or manipulation has occurred. At least this is so insofar as we are dealing with private actors.

Meta, as Facebook is now called, significantly changed its practice in 2020.[21] The 2020 approach applied broadly to video, images, and audio. As Meta explained:

Going forward, we will remove misleading manipulated media if it meets the following criteria:

- *It has been edited or synthesized – beyond adjustments for clarity or quality – in ways that aren't apparent to an average person and would likely mislead someone into thinking that a subject of the video said words that they did not actually say. And:*
- *It is the product of artificial intelligence or machine learning that merges, replaces or superimposes content onto a video, making it appear to be authentic.*

This policy does not extend to content that is parody or satire, or video that has been edited solely to omit or change the order of words.

In 2024, Meta shifted yet again.[22] It decided not to remove manipulated media, but merely to label it. It also decided to apply its policies more broadly, so as to include any images, video, or audio. As Meta put it:

---

[21] Enforcing Against Manipulated Media, Facebook (Jan. 6, 2020), https://about.fb.com/news/2020/01/enforcing-against-manipulated-media/.

[22] Our Approach to Labeling AI-Generated Content and Manipulated Media, Facebook (Apr. 5, 2024), https://about.fb.com/news/2024/04/metas-approach-to-labeling-ai-generated-content-and-manipulated-media/.

If we determine that digitally-created or altered images, video or audio create a particularly high risk of materially deceiving the public on a matter of importance, we may add a more prominent label so people have more information and context. This overall approach gives people more information about the content so they can better assess it and so they will have context if they see the same content elsewhere.

This is not an adequate response! At least in cases of likely harm, removal is the appropriate response. To be sure, Meta's Community Standards do require removal if a deepfake is independently unacceptable – because, for example, it involves bullying, harassment, or nudity. But deepfakes that portray people or events in a misleading light may be strong candidates for removal, at least if they are not parody or satire. To be sure, there are hard line-drawing problems here. The question, signaled above, is what kind of harm they create.

Table 4.1 shows, at a glance, a range of practices as of 2024 (practices are of course frequently changing).

It is important to emphasize that all over the world, both private and public institutions are trying to reduce the risk of deception and manipulation through deepfakes. Artificial intelligence itself can help; indeed it is essential. In Indonesia, for example, USAID assisted in the development of the Misinformation Early Warning System, an artificial intelligence tool that identifies manipulated online content and finds out how it is being spread. The tool helped to identify a bot network, apparently from China, that was using female Western-sounding usernames to promote a positive narrative about the treatment of Uighurs in Xinjiang province. As a result, several social media platforms removed the content. The growing capacity for technology to manipulate information is accelerating, but so is the capacity for technology to detect that manipulation.

Brave New World

Every day, technology is advancing, and before long, technological capabilities will be unimaginably advanced. But let us not lose our moorings in the swirl of daily events. Human psychology

Table 4.1 Social media platforms' policies on manipulated media

	What kind of **manipulation** is covered?	What kind of **media** is covered?	Need to show any risk of **harm**?	**Remedy** for violation?
Meta	1) "…edited or synthesised, beyond adjustments for clarity or quality, in ways that are not apparent to an average person"; *and* 2) "…the product of **artificial intelligence**[1] or machine learning, including deep learning techniques (e.g. a technical deepfake), that merges, combines, replaces and/or superimposes content…, creating [media] that appears authentic."	*Old policy*: **video** only *New Policy*: **video, images, and audio**	None	Labeling
TikTok	AI-generated *or* "edited" to "show[] realistic-appearing scenes or people."	"[C]ontent, including images, video, or audio"	**None** (but assumption of harm for banned categories[2])	*Most cases*: **Labeling** *Special cases*:[2] **Removal**
X	1) "significantly and deceptively altered, manipulated, or fabricated"; *or*	**Any media** ("Includ[es] images, videos, audios, gifs, and URLs hosting relevant content")	"likely to result in widespread confusion on public issues, impact	*Most cases*: **Labeling** (or showing warnings to people who like/share the post, reducing post

			visibility, and turning off likes/comments) *Special cases* (cases involving "a serious risk of harm to individuals or communities"): **Removal**
	2) "**shared in a deceptive manner** with false content."		public safety, *or* cause serious harm"
YouTube	"technically manipulated or doctored in a way that misleads users (usually beyond clips taken out of context)"	"Content"	"may pose a serious risk of **egregious harm**"	Removal

Notes: The quotes are taken from: Meta: Monika Bickert, Enforcing Against Manipulated Media, Facebook (Jan. 6, 2020), https://about.fb.com/news/2020/01/enforcing-against-manipulated-media [https://perma.cc/A4SV-878X]; TikTok: Misleading and False Content, TikTok (Last updated – Nov. 2024), https://ads.tiktok.com/help/article/tiktok-ads-policy-misleading-and-false-content#anchor-1-0; X: Yoel Roth and Ashita Achuthan, Building Rules in Public: Our Approach to Synthetic & Manipulated Media, X Blog (Feb. 4, 2020), https://blog.x.com/en_us/topics/company/2020/new-approach-to-synthetic-and-manipulated-media; YouTube: Misinformation Policies, YouTube Help (2024), https://support.google.com/youtube/answer/10834785?hl=en.

[1] It is possible the new policy will cover a broader swath of manipulated media, but Meta's blog posts suggest that it will be limited to AI-generated content.

[2] AI-generated content or edited media will be removed if it falsely shows: (1) Content made to seem as if it comes from an authoritative source, such as a reputable news organization; (2) A crisis event, such as a conflict or natural disaster; *or* (3) A public figure who is: (a) being degraded or harassed, or engaging in criminal or anti-social behavior; (b) taking a position on a political issue, commercial product, or a matter of public importance (such as an election); *or* (c) being politically endorsed or condemned by an individual or group.

stays constant, or pretty close to it, and the same is true for the underlying principles.

Deepfakes are a clear and present danger to individual autonomy, to the integrity of reputations, to commerce, to politics, and to democracy. They are often deceptive. They are often manipulative. Where they cause serious harm, they should not be allowed.

5 SCARCITY AND ATTENTION: MANIPULATED BY SLUDGE

Magicians manipulate people. They trick the eye. They focus your attention on one location, while diverting your attention from another, which is where the real action is. They are masters at that.

Have a look at *The Prestige*, the amazing 2006 film by Christopher Nolan. It is a tale of a fierce competition between two magicians: Alfred Bordon, played by Christian Bale, and Robert Angier, played by Hugh Jackman. Things go sour when Borden accidentally causes the death of Angier's wife (played by Piper Perabo), leading to a competition between the two magicians, essentially to the death. (Or is it?) Bordon and Angier have plenty of tricks. Typically they fool people by exploiting the fact of limited attention.

Limited attention comes in turn from *cognitive scarcity*, which makes us susceptible to being manipulated. A little sludge makes things much worse, and magicians introduce various kinds of sludge. But I am getting ahead of the story.

Online sellers are not magicians, at least not technically, but they have a magic of their own. A number of years ago, American Express made me an offer: I could receive, for free, a subscription to six magazines. That sounded like a good deal. (Free magazines!) Of the magazines they offered, I loved exactly none, but I could find six that seemed fine, and I chose them. A decade later, I was still receiving the magazines. Working at the time on the topic of behavioral economics, I decided to investigate. It turned out that for nine years and nine months, I had been paying for magazines that I didn't like. I just hadn't been paying attention to the fact that the "free subscription" offer meant three months of free magazines. After that, you would be automatically billed, unless you canceled. Who knew? I didn't. American Express aimed to manipulate me, and it succeeded.

More recently, I told this tale to an audience of business types, which included someone who helped run a weekly magazine. He came up to me afterwards and said, "We know all about this. If we automatically renew people's subscriptions, our renewal rate is amazingly high – over 90 percent. If we ask people to say whether they want to renew, well, we lose a lot of money."

When I was writing this book, I was fortunate enough to be asked to give a lecture at a well-known university. The lecture came with an honorarium – certainly not huge, but not tiny. To my surprise, the university sent me a link to something called a Service Portal, and asked me to register as a "supplier." The portal was so complicated, and so hard to navigate, that I gave up trying to use it. So did my superb assistant. After repeated online requests from the university, and unfriendly notes (from artificial intelligence?), I saw no option but to offer to give the lecture for free.

Now consider the following cases:

1. A cell phone company markets many of its phones with mail-in rebates. Consumers are entitled to a rebate of $200. The company is well aware that many consumers will be excited about the potential rebate – and that they will fail to mail in the forms. The company is pleased by that fact.
2. Consumers can subscribe to programming from Amazing Science Fiction Network, a television network; the subscription gives them access to a great deal of programming, including shows that are not available on television. Obtaining a subscription is easy. It is essentially one-click. Canceling a subscription is not so easy. It requires a telephone call with a significant waiting time and a series of questions (perhaps from space aliens), nominally designed to ensure that people really do want to cancel.
3. To obtain benefits under a health care law, people must navigate a complicated website. Many of them do not understand the

questions that they are being asked. For many people, the application takes a long time. Some of them give up.
4. To register a complaint about defective automobiles, consumers are required by law to fill out lengthy online forms. The forms require detailed information about where the vehicle was originally purchased and how it was used. Some consumers do not have easy access to that information. Others fear that their privacy might be invaded. Many of them decide not to fill out the forms at all.
5. Whenever people visit certain websites, they are informed of the privacy policies of those sites, and if they want to proceed, they are asked to check a box, indicating that they consent. Sometimes the legally mandatory notice is in an unfamiliar language.

All of these cases involve *sludge*: "a viscous mixture," in the form of administrative burdens or frictions that make it difficult for consumers, employees, employers, students, patients, clients, small businesses, and many others to get what they want or to do as they wish. Imposition of sludge can be a form of manipulation. Sometimes it is even magical.

By imposing sludge, public and private institutions can impose a lot of frustration and make it hard for people to make a reflective and deliberative choice. Often sludge is invisible; people did not consent to it. Sludge can make an interaction, online or in person, very different from what people expected and wanted it to be.

I have three goals in this chapter. The first is to elaborate the idea of sludge, with close reference to behavioral economics. As we will see, sludge is an exceedingly effective way of manipulating people. The second is to give an account of why sludge can be so harmful to consumers, students, patients, clients, investors, workers, and others, with reference to behavioral findings about present bias, inertia, limited attention, and unrealistic optimism. Private and public institutions sometimes have a strong interest in increasing sludge – and sometimes have a strong interest in reducing it.

The third goal is to call for regular Sludge Audits by both the private and public sectors. The purpose of Sludge Audits is to produce clarity about the magnitude of sludge and to ensure transparency to people who are affected by it, including those who are in a position to reduce sludge. As a result of that transparency, Sludge

Audits should motivate a careful assessment, in law and policy, of how to reduce sludge – and a pervasive form of manipulation, especially of consumers.

It is important to note that Sludge Audits can be more or less formal and elaborate. They might be highly quantitative, embodying an effort to calculate both costs and benefits. They might be more qualitative, with an effort to understand what is being required and to ask, in a more intuitive way, whether the existing levels of sludge are excessive. In either case, they should be seen as part of a general effort to enlist behavioral findings in an effort to simplify law, government, and policymaking.

A Glimpse

For a preliminary glimpse of the potential benefits of Sludge Audits, consider the Transportation Security Administration (TSA) Precheck Program, designed to speed up security lines at airports. The program, adopted by the United States in 2011, followed a kind of Sludge Audit; it was based on the conclusion that the standard security processes are excessively burdensome for many travelers. Those enrolled in the program are able to take advantage of expedited screening and shorter lines – a clear effort at sludge reduction. In a recent year, 20 million people were enrolled. What are its benefits?

Let us assume, conservatively, that on average, those 20 million people use the program four times per year. If so, we are speaking of 80 million uses. Let us also assume, plausibly, that on average, a user of the program saves twenty minutes per trip. If so, we are speaking of roughly 1.6 billion minutes saved per year. Let us assume, finally, that an hour is worth, on average, $30. If so, the benefit of the TSA program is at least $48 billion per year. To do a full analysis of the welfare effects of the program, of course, we would need to know the costs as well. Setting up and administering the program requires significant resources. But it is safe to say that, once the program is up and running, the net benefits are very high.

Security lines are not exactly manipulative, and some sludge is not a form of manipulation. Still, the example is illustrative. Whenever a specified amount of time is saved by a large population of consumers – say 200,000 hours – the benefits will not exactly be trivial. Importantly, monetizing time savings is hardly sufficient to capture those benefits. Some of the benefits of sludge reduction are psychological and hedonic – a reduction of frustration, anxiety, and perhaps a sense of stigma or humiliation. In addition, sludge reduction efforts can greatly improve access to goods and services, including permits, licenses, antipoverty programs, education, job training, and economic opportunities.

For consumers, students, and employees, such efforts can change lives. For companies, they can increase sales and good-will. For governments, they can greatly improve performance. They can promote economic development and growth. In many contexts, efforts to reduce sludge will have disproportionate benefits for the most disadvantaged members of society; they can be an engine of opportunity. Diverse nations, concerned about poverty and education, would do well to conduct Sludge Audits – and to prioritize sludge reduction.

Sludge as Manipulation

If sludge is understood to consist of administrative burdens or frictions, the concept is not exactly mysterious. The term should be taken to refer to the kind of friction, large or small, that people face when they want to go in one or another direction. For their own reasons, whether self-interested or altruistic, private and public institutions might impose or increase sludge. In the private sector, companies can use sludge to increase profits. For example, people might want to cancel a subscription to a magazine in which they no longer have the slightest interest, but to do that, they might have to wade through a great deal of sludge. That is a way of manipulating people. Online sludge is a kind of dark pattern; it is a way to steer people toward outcomes that take their time or their money.

In the public sector, sludge may be an accident, but it might also be a deliberate choice, in which case it might count as a form of manipulation. People might want to sign their child up for some beneficial program, such as free transportation or free school meals, but the sludge might defeat them. Maybe it is intended to do that. The right to vote may be the most fundamental of all, but a sludge-filled registration process might disenfranchise many millions of people. It might also be manipulative, a form of trickery designed to prevent people from making reflective choices. A sludge reduction initiative might be a Voting Rights Act. To obtain financial aid for college, students in the United States are required to fill out the Free Application for Federal Student Aid (FAFSA). Until recently, it was long and complicated, and it required young people to provide information that they might not have (some of it is on their parents' tax returns). Many students gave up. That might have been the goal.

For conceptual clarity, we should not consider monetary incentives or disincentives to be sludge. If consumers are told that they must pay a specified amount to obtain insurance or that they can obtain a better seat on an airplane for a small additional fee, they are facing costs, not sludge. A legal ban is not sludge: If people are forbidden to smoke in public places, sludge is not the problem. A legal mandate may or may not be sludge, depending on what is mandated. If people are told that they have to go through an unnecessarily complex process to get help with depression or anxiety, they are certainly being required to wade through sludge. If people are told that they must obtain health insurance, the same conclusion holds to the extent that obtaining health insurance involves a great deal of friction.

From one point of view, of course, there is no real distinction between monetary incentives and the kinds of costs imposed by sludge. After all, time can be monetized, and if the costs are emotional or hedonic, they can be monetized as well. A monetary cost of a specified low amount is less than a time cost of a specified high amount. If we believe that costs are simply costs, then sludge might be characterized as a kind of cost, whose magnitude can be quantified and monetized.

The only response is that qualitative distinctions are useful, and there is an important qualitative distinction between (say) a tax or a fine on the one hand and a pointless form-filling requirement on the other. From the public sector, sludge is often an indirect, covert, and inadequately scrutinized method of achieving particular policy goals, by limiting access to various programs and benefits; a spotlight should be placed on that method.

Sludge is bad if and when it imposes *excessive* frictions. It should be clear that frictions or administrative burdens, imposed by private or public institutions, can be excessive, insufficient, or optimal. If people are asked whether they are sure that they want to delete some important file, waive their legal rights, send an angry email, or post something on social media, the resulting burdens might be an effort to prevent mistakes or recklessness. A mandatory cooling-off period for door-to-door sales, of the sort imposed by the Federal Trade Commission in 1972, is an example. So is a waiting period before people can buy guns. "Are-You-Sure-You-Want-To" questions can provide both individual and social benefits. A waiting period can even be a way of weakening the effect of an effort at manipulation. In due course, I shall provide an account of the legitimate reasons for sludge.

Why Sludge Matters

It should be clear that those who impose sludge might do so intentionally or inadvertently. From the moral point of view, intentional imposition of sludge may be especially objectionable. Those who impose sludge are often attempting to promote self-interested goals. Imposition of sludge is often a form of manipulation, as, for example, when companies try to exploit inertia or present bias so as to lead people to buy unduly costly products or plans. When imposition of sludge is inadvertent, it should not be seen as a form of manipulation – but it might still be bad. It might be a product of official cluelessness, as, for example, when bureaucrats or lawyers impose administrative burdens that turn out to have serious or even devastating adverse effects, even though those who designed them intended no such thing. Even if the benefits of sludge are high, its costs might prove overwhelming.

These costs can take qualitatively different forms. They might involve the acquisition of *information*, which might be difficult and expensive to obtain. They might involve *time*, which people might not have. They might be *psychological*, in the sense that they involve frustration, stigma, or humiliation. (People who are poor, elderly, or disabled may feel especially frustrated, stigmatized, or humiliated.) When any of these costs are high, it might be very difficult to navigate or overcome sludge. In some cases, doing relevant paperwork might be literally impossible; it simply may not be feasible for people to obtain the information to enable them to fill out the forms, or to learn how to do that. By themselves, these points help explain the low take-up rates for many federal and state programs, as well as the immense difficulty that people often have in obtaining permits or licenses of various sorts.

We should even see sludge as an obstacle to freedom, especially insofar as it reduces or impairs navigability. Freedom of choice

Figure 5.1 SiriusXM Cancellation
Source: Deceptive Patterns, Hall of Shame, www.deceptive.design/hall-of-shame.

is important, but if people cannot get where they want to go, they are not exactly free. Sludge can operate in the same way as coercion. It creates walls and barriers.

We have seen that one kind of dark pattern consists of "roach motel": easy to get in, hard to get out. That is a form of manipulation. Figure 5.1 shows an image from SiriusXM that requires customers to call (and sometimes wait on hold) to cancel their subscriptions, which represents a challenge faced by subscribers to many products and services.

In the United States, the important 2024 "time is money" initiative,[1] attacking manipulation, was explicitly designed to forbid this kind of practice.

---

[1] www.whitehouse.gov/briefing-room/statements-releases/2024/08/12/fact-sheet-biden-harris-administration-launches-new-effort-to-crack-down-on-everyday-headaches-and-hassles-that-waste-americans-time-and-money/.

Unredeemable Sludge and Manipulation

An assortment of human biases amplify the real-world effects of sludge. For many people, inertia is a powerful force, and people tend to procrastinate. If people suffer from inertia, and if they procrastinate, they might never do the necessary paperwork. The problem is compounded by present bias. When sludge is intentional, it exploits human biases, and is manipulative for that reason.

To understand why sludge matters, let us note that for many of us the future often seems like a foreign country – Laterland – that we are not sure we will ever visit. It is often tempting to put off administrative tasks until another day. That day may never come, even if the consequences of delay are quite serious. Those who impose sludge are often gleefully aware of that point.

To see the point, consider mail-in forms, unquestionably a form of sludge. Such forms provide people with an opportunity to obtain some kind of gain, often in the form of a check, but they require people to overcome inertia. An illustration of the relationship among behavioral biases, sludge, and manipulation comes from a study of people's failure to redeem such forms, with a memorably precise name: Everyone Believes in Redemption.[2]

Across various markets, redemption rates usually range between 10 percent and 40 percent, which means that a strong majority of customers forget or simply do not bother. Because of the power of inertia, that might not be terribly surprising. What is more striking is the finding that people are unrealistically optimistic about the likelihood that they will ever redeem forms. In the relevant study, people thought that there was about an 80 percent chance that they would do so within the thirty days they were given. The actual redemption rate was 31 percent. It is an overstatement to say that everyone believes in redemption – but most people certainly do.

In the same study, the researchers made three efforts (with different groups of people) to reduce the massive difference between the predicted and actual redemption rates. First, they informed participants, very clearly, that in previous groups with similar

---

[2] Joshua Tasoff and Robert Letzler, Everyone Believes in Redemption: Nudges and Overoptimism in Costly Task Completion, 107 *J. of Economic Behavior & Organization* 107 (2014).

people, redemption rates were below one-third. Second, they issued two clear reminders, one soon after purchase and another when the deadline for redemption was near. Third, they made redemption far simpler by eliminating the requirement that people must print out and sign a certification page.

As it turned out, not one of the three interventions reduced people's optimism! In all conditions, people thought there was about an 80 percent chance that they would mail in the forms. Moreover, and somewhat surprisingly, the first two interventions had no effect on what people actually did. When hearing about the behavior of other groups, people apparently thought, "Well, those are *other* groups. What do they have to do with us?" In other contexts, reminders often work because they focus people's attention and reduce the power of inertia. But in this case, reminders turned out to be useless.

The only effective intervention was simplification, which had a strong impact on what people actually did. By making it easier to mail in the form and thus reducing sludge, simplification significantly increased people's willingness to act. The redemption rate rose to about 54 percent, which means that the disparity between belief and behavior was cut in half. Here, then, is concrete evidence of the potentially significant effect of sludge reduction in increasing people's access to valuable benefits. It is worth considering, in a context like this one, whether legal reform is a good idea.

Behavioral Biases, Manipulation, and Sludge

Recall that inertia is a powerful force and that, because of inertia, people might not fill out necessary forms or otherwise navigate sludge. That is one reason that participation rates are often much lower with opt-in designs than with opt-out designs. Recall too that inertia is aggravated by present bias, leading people to focus on the short term and neglect the future. Suppose in this light that consumers must fill out certain forms in order to be eligible for important benefits or to avoid significant penalties. They might intend to do exactly that, but if the task can be put off, or if it is burdensome or difficult, their behavior might not match their intentions. The actual costs might turn out to be very high; the perceived costs might be far higher. More generally, sludge has a significant impact that many people do not foresee. As the redemption study shows, people are unrealistically optimistic about the likelihood that they will overcome inertia. Even specialists might be surprised at the extent to which apparently promising strategies fail.

In this light, sludge can be used opportunistically by manipulative marketers who seek to give consumers the impression that they will receive an excellent deal but who know that consumers will not take advantage of the opportunity. In some cases, government officials are doing the same thing. They are proclaiming the availability of some benefit, or masking their efforts to reduce its availability, all the while using sludge opportunistically. Alternatively, or perhaps at the same time, they might be responding to political values and commitments. Officials might use sludge as a rationing device or as a way of conserving taxpayer resources. In some cases, sludge has a damaging effect that officials do not anticipate. In particular, private and public institutions might not understand the extent to which sludge will adversely affect a population that they are seeking to help. Behavioral biases might make administrative burdens essentially prohibitive or impose a serious challenge in terms of navigability; people in the private or public sector might fail to anticipate that.

Consider the effort required to unsubscribe to promotional emails. Everyone loves Canada (or should, as I certainly do), but Air Canada appears to leverage sludge and inertia to capture an audience by making opting into promotional emails automatic and mandatory when purchasing a ticket online (see Figure 5.2).

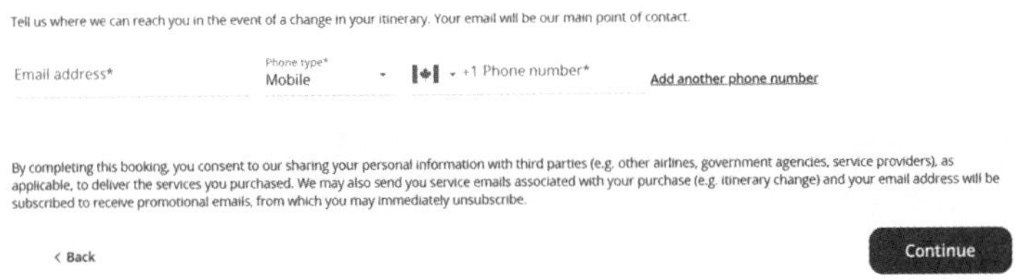

Figure 5.2 Air Canada promotional emails
Source: Deceptive Patterns, Hall of Shame, www.deceptive.design/hall-of-shame.

Scarcity

With respect to redemption, the power of simplification puts a new spotlight on the large consequences of seemingly modest sludge – on the effects of choice architecture in determining outcomes. Simplification and burden reduction do not merely reduce frustration; they can change people's lives. An underlying reason is that our cognitive resources are limited. Inevitably, we are able to focus on only a small subset of life's challenges. For those who are busy, poor, disabled, or elderly, the problem of cognitive scarcity is especially serious.[3] For that reason, it is important to focus on the *distributional* effects of sludge – on whom it is most likely to hurt. Used to manipulate people, sludge can most injure those who are at the bottom of the social and economic ladder.

As a practical matter, the burden of sludge, imposed by law, is often borne principally by poor people, and that is a burden that they cannot readily bear. A central reason is that by virtue of their poverty, poor people must focus on a wide range of immediately pressing problems. If a private or public institution is asking poor people to navigate a complex system or to fill out a lot of forms, they might give up. But the problem is hardly limited to the poor. When programs are designed to benefit the elderly, sludge might be especially damaging, at least if the population suffers from reduced cognitive capacity. Something similar can be said for immigrants or for people who suffer from a language barrier. For different reasons, the problem of sex equality deserves particular attention. Because women do a disproportionate amount of administrative work – running the household, arranging meals, taking care of children – a significant reduction in sludge could address a pervasive source of social inequality, with ramifying effects on other areas of life.

Justifying Sludge

Notwithstanding what I have said thus far, sludge can serve important goals. It might help consumers, patients, students, and employees. It can sometimes be justified on welfare grounds. It need

---

[3] Sendhil Mullainathan and Eldar Shafir, *Scarcity: Why Having So Little Means So Much* (2013).

not be manipulative. In some ways, it can even increase people's autonomy.

Self-Control Problems

We have seen that sludge might be designed to counteract self-control problems, recklessness, and impulsivity. It can be a way of protecting people against their own errors. It can strengthen the hand of the planner in the face of an insufficiently deliberative doer. For that reason, it can work as a nudge, curing a behavioral problem. Nudges are defined as *freedom-preserving interventions that steer people in a particular direction*. For example, a warning is a nudge, and so is a little friction (for much more detail, see Chapters 7 and 8).

For mundane decisions, nudges are frequently encountered online, with questions asking whether consumers "are sure that they want to" send an email without a subject line, cancel a recent order, or delete a file. Such nudges can be an excellent idea, and they need not be manipulative. Similar nudges, imposed by private and public institutions, might make sense for life-altering decisions, such as marriage and divorce. Cooling-off periods can be a blessing. Consider the case of gun purchases, where waiting periods save lives.

Privacy and Security

Private and public institutions often impose sludge in order to obtain information about people's backgrounds – their employment history, their income, their criminal history (if any), their credit rating, their family history, their places of residence. Those who seek to work in government, certainly at levels that involve national security, are required to provide a great deal of information of that sort. (I have had several such positions in government, and while the sludge is not a lot of fun, it is justified.) It is at least reasonable to think that if private and public institutions are to receive some or all of that information, it must be with people's explicit consent. If so, the question is whether to ask people to face administrative burdens or instead to intrude on their privacy. Perhaps it is not so terrible if officials choose the former. Here again, there is no problem of manipulation.

At one time, of course, officials had no real option. They could not intrude on privacy because they lacked the means to do so. Increasingly, however, private and public institutions actually have independent access to that information, or they might be able to obtain it with a little effort online. But would that be desirable? Not necessarily. In some cases, there is a tradeoff between irritating burdens on the one hand and potential invasions of privacy on the other. Consider, for example, the question of how much information credit card companies should acquire before offering cards to customers. We might welcome situations in which such companies can learn what is required and simply send people offers or even cards. Whether we should do so depends in part on what information they have and whether it might be misused. If government has, or acquires, the relevant information, the risks might be thought unacceptable.

The question of security is closely related. To set up an online account, consumers might be asked to provide, and might be willing to provide, sensitive information – involving, for example, their bank account or their credit card. People might have to answer questions about their address, their social security number, or their mother's maiden name. Forcing people to answer these questions can be a bother, but it is not manipulative, and it might be justified as a means of ensuring against some kind of breach.

Ideally, of course, we would have some clarity about the benefits and costs of obtaining the relevant information. But if costs and benefits are difficult to specify, it might make sense to have a rough-and-ready sense that not-especially-onerous burdens are desirable to prevent the worst-case scenarios in terms of privacy and security.

Acquiring Useful Data

Companies and governments might seek to acquire data that can be used for multiple purposes, and that might benefit the public a great deal. For example, companies might want to know a great deal about consumers, so as to be able to serve them better. Or officials might want to know whether people who receive employment training, or some kind of educational funding, are actually benefiting from the relevant program. What do they do with that training or that funding?

Those who receive information-collection requests might complain of sludge. But the relevant burdens might be justified as a means of ensuring acquisition of important or even indispensable knowledge. In the modern era, acquisition of information might promote public and private accountability. It might save money. It might spur innovation. It might even save lives. It need not manipulate anyone.

Eligibility and Qualifications

When private and public institutions impose sludge, one reason may involve eligibility restrictions; another may involve record-keeping. Those who seek a loan, private or public, must fill out forms. The central reason is to ensure that, as a matter of law, they actually qualify! People should not receive government benefits unless they are entitled to them under the law.

It is true that with the increasing availability of information and with machine learning, private and public institutions might be able to find the relevant information on their own. In the private sector, some companies use the idea of "prequalification," which means that they have enough information to know, in advance, that some people are already qualified for goods or services. Sometimes forms can be "prepopulated"; as a result, a lot of form-filling might not be necessary. In the domain of taxation, one example is the idea of return-free filing, which eliminates the need for taxpayers to fill out forms at all. In the fullness of time, we should see significant movements in this direction. But those movements remain incipient.

The most obvious explanation for sludge goes by the name of "program integrity." Suppose that the Internal Revenue Service decided to send the Earned Income Tax Credit to apparently eligible taxpayers. If it could do so at low cost, and if the apparently eligible taxpayers are in fact eligible, there would be little ground for objection. The problem, of course, is the word "apparently." It is possible that some of the recipients will not in fact be eligible. Whenever people are automatically enrolled in a program, some of them may not meet the legal criteria.

When this is so, regulators must choose between (1) a design ensuring that some eligible people will not receive a benefit and (2) a design ensuring that some ineligible people will receive a benefit.

If the idea of program integrity is meant to refer to the number of errors, the choice between (1) and (2) might turn purely on arithmetic: Which group is larger? If automatic enrollment means that 500,000 eligible people receive the benefit who otherwise would not, that's a very good thing, and if sludge would prevent just 50 ineligible people from receiving the benefit, automatic enrollment would seem justified.

But if we play with the numbers, we could imagine reasonable disagreements. Suppose that automatic enrollment gives benefits to 200,000 eligible people who would otherwise not receive them, but also to 200,001 ineligible people who would also otherwise not receive them. That would seem pretty terrible. So many people are getting the money who are not eligible for it! But some people might think that if the 200,001 people are nearly eligible – if they are relatively poor – it is not all that terrible if they receive some economic help. Other people might think that taxpayer money is accompanied by clear restrictions, and if it is given out in violation of those restrictions, a grave wrong has been committed – which means that even a very modest breach of program integrity, for the advantage of those who are not eligible, is unacceptable.

The most extreme version of this view would be that a grant of benefits to a very large number of eligibles would not compensate for the grant of benefits to a very small number of ineligibles. From a welfarist standpoint, the most extreme version is hard to defend: A grant of benefits to ten people who are almost (but not quite) eligible would seem to be a price worth paying in return for a grant of benefits to a million people who are in fact eligible. But the correct tradeoff is not self-evident. Here again, we need not be dealing with manipulation at all.

Sludge Audits

I have emphasized that the problem of sludge outruns the problem of manipulation, but one way to combat manipulation is to conduct regular Sludge Audits. Let's explore them, in part to reduce manipulation, but more broadly to make life easier and better.

Governments should certainly be conducting such audits. The same is true of a wide assortment of private institutions. Banks, insurance companies, hospitals, universities, online sellers, and publishers could save a great deal of money by reducing sludge, and they could greatly improve the experience of people who interact with them. They might even be able to change people's lives. It is worth underscoring the case of hospitals, where sludge can not only create immense frustration but also impair health and even cost lives. A Sludge Audit overlaps with a Dark Patterns Audit, because many dark patterns enlist sludge.

We have seen that Sludge Audits can take both formal and informal forms. They might involve a great deal of quantification, or they might be more qualitative. In either case, three reforms would do a great deal to improve the current situation. First, institutions should undertake a periodic "lookback" at existing burdens to see if the current "stock" can be justified and to eliminate those that turn out to be outmoded, pointless, or too costly. This reform would build on existing lookback requirements for regulation in general. Second, institutions should choose the least burdensome method for achieving their goals. This is essentially a requirement of cost-effectiveness. If, for example, annual reporting would be as effective as quarterly reporting, then agencies should choose annual reporting. Third, institutions should ensure that the benefits of sludge justify the costs.

It is true and important that cost-benefit balancing is not always simple for sludge. Quantification might be challenging; monetary equivalents might be difficult to devise. In such cases, a crude approach would be to understand the requirement of cost-benefit justification not as an effort to compare social costs and social benefits, understood in economic terms, but instead as entailing a more intuitive assessment of *proportionality*. Is a lot of sludge being imposed, and if so, is it likely to serve significant purposes? Can we say anything about the actual magnitude of the costs and the magnitude of the gains? Real numbers would help inform decisions and combat sludge, but we should be able to make a lot of progress without them.

It is worth emphasizing the fact that even a crude form of cost-benefit analysis would be *information forcing*. It would create a clear incentive to have accurate accounts of the number of hours of work required by current levels of sludge, and also to turn those hours into monetary equivalents. It would simultaneously create an incentive for institutions to be more specific, and more quantitative, about the expected benefits of sludge.

In the easiest cases, Sludge Audits would immediately show institutions, both public and private, that the existing level of sludge is not in their interests – and that it is harming or manipulating people. With respect to the public sector: If it turns out to be difficult for children to get access to free school meals, simply because the sludge is excessive, officials might take steps to reduce it. If it turns out to be hard for students to obtain financial aid, because the forms have more than 100 questions, an understanding of that fact might produce an effort to cut the number of questions. If it turns out that needy families have a hard time receiving food to which they have a legal right, sludge reduction, perhaps through the use of online services, might seem quite appealing. If it turns out that building permits take immense time and effort to obtain, and if that time and effort contributes to housing shortages, efforts to reduce the necessary time and effort might be met with general applause.

With respect to the private sector: If it turns out to be difficult for consumers to do what must be done to buy a product – say, an automobile – a company might simplify the experience. Doing so might attract more customers and produce a wide range of reputational benefits. Company leaders might well learn that much sludge is an exercise in manipulation. It is not exactly news that consumers will have a far worse experience with a company if it is difficult to learn or understand the terms of an agreement, or to obtain a response to their complaints. Many companies have innovated creatively in an effort to reduce such problems. We could easily imagine a kind of competition to be a sludge-free government or company with respect to everything that matters to citizens or consumers. The same could be true for employees, investors, and students.

At the opposite pole, public or private institutions might know, or learn, that sludge is in their interest, and a Sludge Audit would not create an incentive to reduce it. If sludge discourages immigration, some officials would be pleased to impose sludge, and perhaps to increase it. If sludge reduces entry into certain professions, officials, attuned to the interests of existing entrants, might not be so displeased. It might well be good business to make it very easy to start a subscription – and sludgy to stop. Careful testing might show that such a strategy is optimal. A complaint process that involves a degree of sludge might not merely filter out unjustified complaints; it might also save money when complaints are justified.

Under imaginable circumstances, sludge is in the competitive interest of firms; that is why it exists. Dark patterns make money. If so, the question remains: Is this a kind of behavioral market failure for which a regulatory response is appropriate? The answer will often be "yes." Recall the 2024 Time Is Money initiative,[4] which is full of regulatory responses to sludge.

The largest point is that, for public institutions, a Sludge Audit will often reveal that there are significant opportunities for improving performance. Every year, for example, the U.S. government is required to publish something like a Sludge Audit: The Information Collection Budget (ICB) of the United States. The ICB quantifies the annual paperwork burden that the U.S. government imposes on its citizens. In recent years, the annual number is in the vicinity of 10 billion hours! In spite of significant shifts, the burden has been high for a long time. The ICB also offers details across agencies, showing, among other things, that the Department of Treasury is responsible for well over half of the total.

It should not be difficult for governments all over the world to produce an ICB, cataloguing paperwork burdens. To be sure, some of those burdens are undoubtedly justified. In addition, the worst forms of sludge might not be paperwork at all (consider time waiting in line). But for governments, an ICB is an important start, not least because it is likely to spur sludge reduction efforts. Private institutions should be producing similar documents, if only for internal use; and public transparency might well be a good idea.

Organizations dedicated to economic growth, public health, good education, clean air and clean water, sex equality, voting rights, poverty reduction, and prosperous small businesses and start-ups do not now march under banners stating, "Sludge Reduction Now!" But time is the most valuable commodity that human beings have. We should be working to find ways to give them more of it.

---

[4] *See* Chapter 3.

6 THE BARBIE PROBLEM: MANIPULATED BY SOCIAL PRESSURE

Now let us approach the problem of manipulation from a very different angle. In this chapter, we will not be dealing with hidden or covert influences, which have been my main focus thus far. We will not be dealing with magic or sludge. Instead we will be focusing on how social dynamics can lead people to make choices that they deplore. Clever marketers, including public officials, often manipulate people through the strategic use or exploitation of such dynamics. This is a different kind of trickery.

The basic problem is that *people can be manipulated into buying goods that they wish did not exist.* They buy those goods not because they really like them, but because of the social signals that they give, or the social losses that they incur, if they do not buy them.

Online, that is happening every day. Call it the Barbie Problem.

Bad Goods

Notwithstanding the success of the terrific 2023 movie, and with apologies to anyone who really does love Barbie, I speculate that many children, and even more parents, wish that there was no such thing as Barbie. (If you don't agree with my speculation, no matter; please indulge me here.) This is so even if children play with Barbie, and even if parents purchase Barbie, and even if children sincerely ask for Barbie. One problem is that not having a Barbie might provide an unwanted signal. Another problem is that not having a Barbie might produce exclusion from a social network.

(I don't like Barbies. I really don't. My older daughter had one, and it gave me the creeps. Okay, that's out of my system.)

As we shall see, Barbies are everywhere. New cell phones may be Barbies. Many online products are Barbies. As we shall also see, social media platforms might themselves be Barbies, at least to many users. Consumers in general, and platform users, are being manipulated by strategic use of social influences.

The Joy of Missing Out

To see the structure of the problem, imagine that there is a party next Saturday night. Imagine too that many of your friends will be there. Imagine finally that you have two options: (1) attend the party or (2) skip the party. Contingent on there being a party, you might choose (1). In fact your preference might be both clear and strong. You might be willing to pay a great deal to attend the party.

At the same time, you might prefer another option: (3) the party does not take place. You might wish, on reflection, that the party had not been arranged in the first place. Or you might hope that the party will be canceled. Your preference ordering is: (3), (1), and (2).

Why is that an imaginable preference ordering? A general answer is "fear of missing out," but that phrase is ambiguous. What does it mean? It is often understood to mean that if you miss something, there is some probability that you will lose something of importance – which suggests that you should prefer (1) to either (2) or (3). That is not the situation on which I am focusing. So the question remains: Why would you prefer (3) to (1), but (1) to (2)? We seem to be speaking of the "joy of missing out."

One possibility is that if you do not attend the party, you will give a signal that you would prefer not to give. The signal might be that you do not like parties, that you do not like your friends, or that you do not like the host. The cost of giving any of those signals might seem very high. You might jeopardize or lose friendships, or compromise relationships. But if the party is canceled, you can avoid an event that you prefer to avoid without giving the undesired signal.

Note that a crucial feature of your thinking is the *social meaning* of failing to attend the party.[1] You might not *intend* the received meaning (you do like your friends; you do like your host), but you have little or no control over it.

This, then, is a possible reason for the preference of (3) to (1), and (1) to (2): The unwanted signal that is given by refusing to go to the party. (Note that a great deal depends on the informational environment in which one is acting. If people know that you like them, but do not like parties, you might be able to say that you are not going to the party without offering the unwelcome signal.)

There is another possibility. You might think that if the party happens, there will be opportunities for relationship-building. You might not much care about those opportunities; if you did, you would not want the party to be canceled. Still, you might think that if *other people take advantage of the opportunities and if you do not, you will be at a comparative disadvantage.*[2] This is one conception of "fear of missing out."

If the party is canceled, you do not have to go, which is good (very good!), and you also will not be at a disadvantage, which is good (very good!) as well. You go to the party to avoid that disadvantage, but without the party, you would be better off. Notice that the person who is having the party might be manipulating people into going by exploiting the social harms that reluctant partygoers would incur if they decline to go. (We will get to consumption and social media in due course.)

Now suppose that you go to the party and they have alcohol. You have two choices: (1) drink or (2) do not drink. You might choose (1), even though you would prefer it if (3) no alcohol is served at the party. You might choose (1) over (2) for the same reason that you went to the party in the first place. A possible problem is the signal of (2). You might fear that people would wonder: Are you an alcoholic? Are you a puritan? Do you hate fun? Why can't you loosen up?

---

[1] *See* Lawrence Lessig, The Regulation of Social Meaning, 62 *U Chicago Law Review* 943 (1995).
[2] *Cf.* Leonardo Bursztyn et al., Status Goods: Experimental Evidence from Platinum Credit Cards, 133 *Quarterly J Economics* 1561 (2018); Roger Mason, Measuring the Demand for Status Goods: An Evaluation of Means-End Chaining and Laddering, 2 *Eur Advances Consumer Research* 78 (1995).

(My wife is Irish, and we visit Ireland every year. I do not much like to drink. When I turn down an offer, I can see that my Irish family is thinking: "Maybe he is an alcoholic!" That's not so good. Or they are thinking: "Maybe he disapproves of drinking. Maybe he is a moralistic jerk." That's worse.)

Now suppose that you are in the midst of a conversation. It is not a terrible conversation. You are not suffering, not at all; it is pleasant enough, even though you are bored and a bit restless. You have two choices: (1) continue the conversation and (2) stop the conversation and move on. You choose (1), even though you would much prefer it if (3) the host interrupted you, such that you had no choice but to stop the conversation.

You might choose (1) over (2) for the same reason that you went to the party in the first place. In fact people often engage in conversations for longer than they wish, perhaps above all because terminating a conversation gives a signal that people do not want to give.[3]

Charities, Politics, More

What is true of purely social events might also be true of charitable or political activities. People can be manipulated into parting with their time or their money. That might be fine, even good. But it might not be.

Suppose that there is a fundraising event on Tuesday night or a protest of some kind. You might show up for one or another, perhaps because you do not want to signal that you do not care about the relevant cause. In the extreme case, you actually do not care about that cause, or perhaps you even despise it.

But the personal costs of not showing up might loom very high. You might wish that the event were not occurring or that it would be canceled. But if it is on, you are there. You might not want to signal to your friends that you do not care about the charity or the cause. You might think: I want that charity to prosper, but I do not want to appear at the event or give money. But if the event is

---

[3] Adam M. Mastroianni et al., Do Conversations End When People Want Them To?, 118 *PNAS* 1 (2021).

occurring, I had better appear and give money. (Perhaps a particular friend is strongly encouraging you to do those things.)

Or you might well focus, in such cases, on self-signaling; you do not want to signal, above all to yourself, that you do not much care about some cause that, on reflection, you approve. What kind of self-image can you retain, if you give yourself that embarrassing or even shameful signal?

Note that in such cases, it is possible that people's desire not to give an unwelcome signal to others or to oneself is solving a collective action problem: *The group benefits from widespread participation even though there is an individual incentive to defect (and stay home)*. A beneficial social norm might be in place: Go to events that involve relevant fundraising activities or protests. On reflection, you might celebrate the norm, even if you wish, in some sense, that the event were not occurring. I will return to this point.

Now suppose that you are not happy with your job and that you have another opportunity that you would prefer. Suppose that you like and admire your boss and your coworkers, which means that you are highly reluctant to quit your job; you would feel guilty and a bit ashamed. You did not want to sever your relationship with them, even if you would like to push a magic button and be working elsewhere. As between quitting your job and continuing, you prefer to continue, because of how you would feel if you quit. But if your position were suddenly terminated, for reasons independent of your performance – if you did not have the option of continuing with your job – you would be happier still.

You might have this preference ordering: (1) your position is terminated; (2) you stay in your job; (3) you leave your job. (For obvious reasons, you do not want option (4), which is to be fired.) Here you are focused on the signal given by leaving, and also the potential rupturing of relationships.

Now imagine that there is a competition of some kind, and you might turn out to be the winner. Suppose that you very much hope that you will win. Suppose that you would pay a great deal to win, and also that you would pay something to have a 1/X chance of winning, even if X is a pretty big number. Even so, it is possible that you would prefer that the competition did not exist. The reason is that you are likely to lose, and if you lose, you will be very sad. It may be that everyone, or almost everyone, who is eligible for the prize feels the same way that you do. The basic problem has to do with competitiveness: Some competitors hate to lose, which means they also do not like to compete; and if a competition is on, they badly want to win.

Now suppose that there is a large wedding, far away from you, and that you have been invited. You might lament the invitation. You might not like the idea of traveling, and you might not like weddings (especially, perhaps, large ones). You might think: For me, the costs of going to that darned wedding greatly outweigh the benefits.

Still, you might go. You might think that if you do not go, you will be giving a terrible signal to the bride and groom, and also, perhaps, to many others. You might wish that you had not been invited to that large wedding – or that a small wedding, not including you, had been planned. As an online example, the message shown in Figure 6.1 might well be taken to highlight Spotify users' fear of missing out.

I know that I have been offering a lot of examples. My goal is to show the structure of the problem, and the variety of Barbies. Of course the examples are not the same, but they are overlapping. The shared characteristic is that they involve some good that people consume, or some activity in which people engage, even though they wish that good or activity did not exist. The reasons for their preference ordering vary. The problem might involve signaling to others; it might involve networks and comparative disadvantage; it might involve self-signaling; it might involve competitiveness.

Figure 6.1 Spotify Fear of Missing Out
Source: Deceptive Patterns, Hall of Shame, www.deceptive.design/hall-of-shame.

(This is not meant as an exhaustive list.) In the background, there might be a manipulator who is pulling people's strings – not by hiding anything, or by appealing to System 1, but by exploiting social influences. We are speaking, in short, of a kind of trap.

Barbies, Manipulation, and Product Traps

A great deal of work attempts to elicit people's valuation of social media platforms. If people in the United States are asked how much they would demand to stay off (say) Instagram or YouTube for a month, they state a significant amount, often in the vicinity of $50 and $100.[4] I have engaged in such studies myself, and I find that for a large number of platforms, the average demand is right around there. Findings of this sort suggest that social media platforms produce a substantial consumer surplus. People are so lucky that such platforms exist! They receive, for free, a product that is worth real money to them.

Instagram has about 2.4 billion users worldwide. If we say that the average user would demand $10 to stay off Instagram for a year (a conservative estimate), Instagram is delivering a staggering $20.4 billion in annual benefits.

But we might want to hesitate before accepting that conclusion. People might demand a great deal to stay off a social media platform for a month, *supposing that everyone else who is relevant will be on that social platform for that month*. But what exactly does that tell us? It might tell us that people benefit from being on the platform, in the sense that it provides them with a variety of goods. It might tell us that people enjoy or otherwise benefit from being part of a network. But does it tell us that they are glad that the platform exists? If they could push a button and abolish the platform, would they do that, if their only concern was their own welfare?

---

[4] *See* Hunt Allcott et al., The Welfare Effects of Social Media, 110 *American Economic Review* 629 (2020); Cass R. Sunstein, Valuing Facebook, 4 *Behavioural Public Policy* 370 (2020). Note that these studies ask how much people would demand to stay off platforms, not how much they would pay to be able to use them. My own research asks both questions, and finds a much lower number for willingness to pay; I explore the reasons for the difference in *ibid*.

Leonardo Bursztyn and collaborators tried to answer that question.[5] They found that on average, users would demand $59 to deactivate TikTok for a month, and $47 to deactivate Instagram for the same period. From those findings, which are broadly consistent with those in other studies, we might conclude that the two platforms make people much better off. But in sharp contrast, users would be willing to *pay* $28 to have all of the world, including themselves, deactivate from TikTok for a month – and $10 to do the same for Instagram.

Almost two-thirds of active TikTok users appear to lose welfare from the existence of the platform! The same is true for almost one-half of active Instagram users.

It appears that *many people would demand significant money to stop using a product that they wish did not exist.* Notably, there is heterogeneity on this count; some people truly gain from the existence of both platforms. But a very large number believe that they lose.

It is important to say that a before-the-fact prediction of the welfare effects of deactivation may not measure the actual welfare effects of deactivation.[6] We do not always know whether a good or an activity will make our lives better. I underestimated the benefits of having my dog. (Her name is Snowy.) I overestimated the benefits of having an extra fan at home. (One fan is just fine.) People might be willing to pay something for a good from which they ultimately lose welfare, even apart from the network effects. People might not be willing to pay something for a good from which they would gain welfare, even apart from the network effects.

But if people are willing to demand payment to give up a good for whose abolition they would also be willing to pay, we have good reason to think that people simultaneously benefit from having access to it, contingent on its existence, and would benefit from

---

[5] Leonardo Bursztyn et al., When Product Markets become Collective Traps: The Case of Social Media (NBER Working Paper No. 31771, 2023).
[6] Daniel T. Gilbert and Timothy D. Wilson, Miswanting: Some Problems in the Forecasting of Future Affective States, in *Feeling and Thinking: The Role of Affect in Social Cognition* 178 (Joseph P. Forgas ed. 2001); Daniel T. Gilbert et al., Immune Neglect: A Source of Durability Bias in Affective Forecasting, 75 *J Personality & Social Psychology* 617 (1998).

eliminating it, if only they could. Bursztyn et al. offer strong evidence on behalf of this conclusion.[7]

Tales of Brave Ulysses

If you fear that you might get addicted to something, you might wish that the product did not exist. You might not want to ban cigarettes, because you might believe that people have a right to smoke. But you might think, on reflection, that it would be better if cigarettes did not exist. You might think that the world would be better if heroin and cocaine were not with us. You might think more broadly that people can be tempted, and that it would be good if some or many sources of temptation had never been invented.

In Chapter 2, we encountered the situation of Ulysses and the Sirens, in which a person takes active steps to protect himself from irresistible temptation. In some cases, people do not want to be subject to certain enticements, which they know they cannot easily resist; they wish that those enticements did not exist, and act to reduce the risk that they will fall victim to them. To say the least, these are important cases. Enticements can be forms of manipulation.

But that is emphatically not the Barbie Problem. In the cases on which I have been focusing, people do not say that they would like to commit themselves in advance not to make certain choices. They *want* to make those choices. The problem is not their own recklessness or impulsiveness, or some form of weakness of will. We are not dealing with a disparity between people's internal "planner," trying to map out a life and people's internal "doer," taking actions from moment to moment. The problem is that not having access to the relevant good creates a loss, *given that the good is available to others*.

The central findings here are in a sense the mirror image of a plausible hypothesis about willingness to pay to protect the environment.[8] Suppose that people are asked how much they are willing to pay to save an endangered species or a pristine area. Suppose too that the amount is trivially small and that if aggregated across a large

---

[7] Leonardo Bursztyn et al., *supra* note 5.
[8] *See* Amartya Sen, Environmental Evaluation and Social Choice: Contingent Valuation and the Market Analogy, 46 *Japanese Economic Review* 23 (1995).

population, it remains relatively small. We might think that people do not much care about the relevant good. But it is possible that people are willing to pay little to protect the environment *unless they are assured that other people will pay as well.* People might think: "My own payment will do little or nothing. But if everyone is paying that admittedly small amount, we can achieve a great deal. I would pay a great deal, supposing that everyone else is doing so."

The Stag Hunt

Return to the example with which I began and suppose that someone has decided to have a party this Saturday night. Suppose that people are willing to go, given that the party is occurring, but that all or most people would prefer that the party not occur. The ambivalent partygoers face a collective action problem known as the stag hunt.[9] If they cannot coordinate, and cannot find a way to agree that they will stay home, they will go to the party. If they can coordinate and agree not to go to the party, they would be better off (unless the signal given by their collective action imposes costs; perhaps the party-giver has power over them). But how can they coordinate? Such coordination might be very difficult, especially if a lot of people have been invited to the party. People might not be able to make credible agreements with one another.

Here is the central point: Companies can maneuver consumers into situations analogous to that of the unwelcome dinner party. That is a form of manipulation. In fact it is pervasive form, even if we do not often notice it.

Suppose, for example, that there is a product that consumers want to have, contingent on its existence, but whose existence consumers do not welcome and might deplore. If so, the product is akin to the Saturday night party. Companies might market a product by emphasizing one of two points: (1) people will feel ashamed or bad if they do not have it (because of the negative signal given by not having it) or (2) people will lose some status by not being part of a network. Plenty of products fall in this category: cars, cell phones, clothing, or laptops. Such products might turn out to be Barbies.

[9] *See* Brian Skryms, *The Stag Hunt and the Evolution of Social Structure* (2004).

Consider wearing ties: Many men have worn ties even though they derive no pleasure from doing so and might wish that ties had never been invented. Ties are Barbies. Or consider high-heeled shoes: Women might wear such shoes even though they find them uncomfortable and wish they did not exist. A great deal of fashion might be characterized as Barbies. Ties and high-heeled shoes are goods that many people buy but wish did not exist.

In some communities, norms have shifted with respect to both of these, and with astonishing rapidity. In some of those communities, men were widely expected to wear ties, but then the COVID-19 pandemic hit, and people worked from home. It seemed kind of dumb to wear a tie while staring into a camera on one's laptop – and men stopped wearing ties. After the end of the pandemic, people returned to the office – and many men did not wear ties. A new and improved equilibrium was established.

Or consider a new iPhone: You might not want to keep using an iPhone from a few years ago, even if you quite like it, if you know that a newer model is available, even if you would be happier if no newer model existed. Bursztyn et al. find evidence consistent with this conclusion.[10] They find that people would prefer less frequent new product launches, even though they would buy the relevant product, given frequent product launches.

The reason for this distribution of preferences is not self-evident. Perhaps people are satisfied with the current product and anticipate (and regret) their own impulsiveness (the Ulysses and the Sirens problem). Perhaps people know that they will be embarrassed for others to see that they do not have the latest model, and so they wish that the latest model were not released so often. New iPhones might be Barbies.

In some of these cases, the structure of the problem is that some person P engages in some action (for example, holds a party, serves alcohol, markets a product) that forces another person Q to make a choice (attend or not, purchase or not) that reveals information about Q that Q does not want to disclose, and that requires Q to decide whether to give a signal that Q would prefer not to give.[11] In many cases, Q's dilemma does not arise by accident. It is a product

---

[10] *See* Bursztyn et al., *supra* note 5.
[11] I am grateful to Eric Posner for focusing on this point.

of P's clever, mischievous, or self-interested action. If P is an employer, it might ask employees to reveal their political leanings, including, for example, whether they would want to unionize. If P is a government, it might give citizens the choice whether to take a loyalty oath (or to decline, politely). These are forms of manipulation.

Norms

I have said that norms often do the work of law; they might prevent people from defecting from some endeavor from which the group benefits.[12] A norm might encourage people to contribute to some shared task – for example, moving office equipment, giving blood, giving to charity, contributing in one or another way to national defense. If the norm were not in place, people might well defect. When a norm solves a collective action problem, it makes people better off, even if each individual would prefer to defect and allow the problem to be solved by others. On reflection, people should welcome the norm.

These cases are important, but they are not my concern here. I am focused on the Barbie Problem – on cases in which people do not, on reflection, welcome the relevant norm. They do not think that it solves a collective action problem. They think that they have been manipulated into, or trapped in, a situation that they dislike or deplore. In some cases, we do have a good or essential norm, not a Barbie Problem. When people go to weddings or funerals to which they wish they had not been invited, they might realize, on reflection, that many or most of us benefit from a norm: If you are invited to a wedding or a funeral, you should probably go. If you go to other people's weddings, you will confer a benefit on the couple and on their friends, and you contribute to the creation of a norm of reciprocity: They will go to your wedding as well. And if you are not going to get married, or are not going to invite them, your attendance contributes to the creation of a kind of social glue.

Something similar can be said about funerals. Many people do not much enjoy going to them (I certainly do not), but they give comfort to people in times of grief, and we all benefit from a norm in

---

[12] *See* Edna Ullmann-Margalit, *The Emergence of Norms* (1977).

favor of comforting the grieving. Funerals are not Barbies, even if you wish you had not been invited.

Positional Goods

There has been a great deal of discussion of the difference between positional and nonpositional goods.[13] When a good is positional, people's enjoyment or experience of it depends on what other people are enjoying or experiencing. When a good is nonpositional, people's enjoyment or experience of it does not depend on what other people are enjoying or experiencing. When a positional good is involved, people can be manipulated. Those who are interested in getting people to buy something, or to do something, might want to emphasize what other people are buying or doing. In many contexts, consumers find themselves on a *positional treadmill*, in which their choices do not really make them happier or better off, but instead serve largely to keep them in the same spot in the hierarchy. You can manipulate people by putting them on a positional treadmill.

Health is plausibly a nonpositional good; people want to be healthy, whether or not most people are healthy. You will not want to have cancer or heart disease, even if a lot of people have cancer or heart disease. Motor vehicles are plausibly positional goods; you might want what now counts as a very good car, or a fancy car, *only because of the current vehicle mix*. This might be true for four different reasons. The first involves signaling: You might want to signal something good about yourself, or at least you might not want to signal something bad about yourself. Motor vehicles are, among other things, signals. The second reason involves your self-image: Even if no one else would know what car you drive, you might not want to think of yourself as the kind of person who drives a less-than-very-good car. The third reason involves envy: You might be envious of people who have a car that is better than yours.

---

[13] *See* Robert H. Frank, Positional Externalities Cause Large and Preventable Welfare Losses, 95 *American Economic Review* 137 (2005); Robert H. Frank, The Demand for Unobservable and Other Nonpositional Goods, 75 *American Economic Review* 101 (1985).

The fourth reason, and the most interesting, is that the current vehicle mix provides *the frame of reference* against which you measure your own car.[14] If the mix were greatly inferior to what it now is, you might like a greatly inferior car; you would not experience it as greatly inferior. But if the mix is much better than it was (say) twenty years ago, your experience of a car from that period would not be very positive. You might find that car to be hopelessly primitive in multiple ways. This is so even if your experience of the car, at the time when it was released, was or would have been exceptionally positive. Positional goods give rise to *positional externalities*: If some people purchase a new car, they impose a cost on those who do not have that car.[15]

Positional goods are among the category of goods that people consume but wish did not exist. Certainly this is true if people consume such goods to avoid giving an unwanted signal, or to avoid a form of unpleasant self-signaling. The frame of reference issue must be analyzed differently. It is hard to unthink what one knows, and if you know about an amazing current motor vehicle, you will not easily wish that everyone had less-than-amazing vehicles from twenty years ago. People can easily be manipulated into thinking that they should buy the latest and the greatest. A key reason is that they can be convinced that their own goods or activities pale in light of what is available, and amazing.

Manipulation and Addiction

Some people struggle with addictions. They might be addicted to cigarettes, alcohol, heroin, or social media. The characteristic feature of an addiction is that people experience (1) lower benefits from consumption over time and (2) higher costs from nonconsumption over time.[16] The first time that you use a drug, you might experience a terrific "high," and if you do not get addicted, you will not suffer if you do not use that drug the next day. The problem is that for some drugs, the "high" is lower the

---

[14] *See* Robert H. Frank, *Luxury Fever* (1999).
[15] *See* Frank, Positional Externalities, *supra* note 13.
[16] *See* Cass R. Sunstein, Legal Interference with Private Preferences, 53 *U Chicago Law Review* 1129, 1159 (1986).

second time (or it takes more to get you to the initial high) – and that a day without the drug may be desperate or miserable, because you crave it. The welfare cost comes because people increasingly suffer from nonconsumption, which means that they wish, on reflection, they had not started consuming the good in the first place.[17] People might even wish that the relevant good did not *exist* in the first place, even as they consume it. Like Ulysses, they might adopt a precommitment strategy to deprive them of access to goods that they would freely choose.

Those who sell addictive goods can be understood as manipulators. They might emphasize the original "high," whatever its source. They might conceal or stay silent about the consequences of addiction. Social media platforms are not exactly drugs, but those who seek to get people addicted to them are very good at their jobs.

All this is true and important, and it has strong implications for law. For example, it supports a ban on smoking,[18] perhaps limited to people born after a certain year,[19] to recognize the current existence of addiction and to prevent further cases of addiction. At one point, New Zealand adopted this strategy, by saying that people born after a particular date could not purchase cigarettes. Although the relevant law was repealed, a lot could be said in its favor. I think it was an excellent idea.

People consume addictive goods even when they wish those goods did not exist in the first place. Addiction is a cousin to my primary interest here, but it is only that. It is not a Barbie Problem.[20] The reason is that once people are addicted, they do not wish that the source of the addiction did not exist. They crave it. True, they wish that they were not addicts, and they might wish that the good

---

[17] We can quibble with this formulation. We need to know more about the benefits and costs of consumption, over time, to know whether people wish, on reflection, that they had not started. Compare a romance with a strong start, a period of addiction, and a terrible end.

[18] *See* Robert Goodin, *No Smoking* (1989).

[19] For an example of this policy, *see* Jessie Gretener and Kathleen Magramo, New Zealand Bans Tobacco Sales for Next Generation, CNN (Dec. 13, 2022), www.cnn.com/2022/12/13/asia/new-zealand-tobacco-ban-intl-hnk/index.html.

[20] By this I mean that people's consumption of addictive goods is not motivated by (1) a desire to avoid signaling or (2) a desire to avoid comparative disadvantages from not consuming addictive goods while everyone else does. At least, let us hope that is the case.

to which they are addicted had not been created in the first place, but these are different kinds of problems. There is a strong argument for regulating addictive goods of all kinds, if and because they reduce people's welfare, and make them less free.

Policy and Law

What are the implications for policy and law? For addictive goods, the answer is relatively well understood. People might be informed or warned; people might be nudged; the relevant goods might be taxed;[21] the relevant goods might be restricted[22] or even banned. For positional goods, the answer is also well understood. Such goods might be taxed,[23] or people might be nudged not to buy them. (More on nudges in Chapters 7 and 8.) A progressive consumption tax might be thought to be the best response to positional externalities.[24] It can reduce the manipulation that can be induced by positional competition.

What about the Barbie Problem? What about goods that people consume so as not to give an unwanted signal, or so as not to be disadvantaged in some network or some status competition? It should be clear that so long as the relevant goods exist, a nudge, a warning, or a tax might not be an adequate response, and might not even be a good idea. Should people really be warned about Barbies, ties, or high heels? Why warn people not to go to parties that they (rationally) want to attend, given the existence of those parties? Should Barbies, ties, or high heels be taxed?

One route for solving the problem lies in voluntary action on the part of those who are stymied or trapped, perhaps through consumer pressures or the creation of a new norm of some kind.

---

[21] *See* Andrew I. Friedson et al., Cigarette Taxes, Smoking, and Health in the Long-Run (NBER Working Paper No. 29145, 2021).
[22] *See* David M. Cutler et al., Economic Approaches to Estimating Benefits of Regulations Affecting Addictive Goods, 50 *American J Preventive Medicine* S20 (2016).
[23] *See* Armenak Antinyan et al., Curbing the Consumption of Positional Goods: Behavioral Intervention versus Taxation, 179 *J Economic Behavior & Organization* 1 (2020); *see also* Frank, Positional Externalities, *supra* note 13 (discussing but rejecting this idea on grounds of administrability).
[24] *See* Frank, Positional Externalities, *supra* note 13.

Perhaps the stag hunt problem can be solved through some kind of cooperation.[25] People might be able to make an agreement and to stick with it. I know someone who adopted a norm in the U.S. government: All meetings will be limited to fifteen minutes. Many people liked that norm. My sister proposed a rule for our family on Christmas: No presents for adults, ever. My family loves that norm.

But in the face of certain kinds of manipulation, producing the Barbie Problem, we could imagine cases in which legal action might be considered. Recall the possibility that some agent has deliberately engineered a situation in which people must either (a) consume a product they do not like or engage in an activity they do not enjoy or (b) offer a signal that they would greatly prefer not to offer, or disclose a fact that they would like to keep private. If the result is to cause serious welfare losses or to intrude on protected rights, legal intervention, perhaps in the form of nudges, ought to be on the table.

An example might be a case in which a public employer gives employees an opportunity to support an incumbent politician, or to come to a holiday celebration associated with a specific religious tradition, or to pray together on Monday mornings. If some action of this kind produces harm, legal intervention ought not to be out of the question – perhaps in the form of nudges, perhaps in the form of taxes, perhaps in the form of subsidies, and perhaps in the form of mandates and bans. In the United States, the Hatch Act can be understood as a specific response to a Barbie Problem: It forbids certain public employees from engaging in political activities, in part because of an understanding that if asked to do so by high-level officials, such employees could not easily refuse. They would be trapped.

Out of Traps

The problem is large and pervasive. Barbies are common. Self-interested actors, online and off, manipulate people by exploiting social influences. In important domains, we would seem to have a basis for rethinking the law of worker and consumer protection

---

[25] A suggestion of collective action, from consumers, is a fair reading of Bursztyn et al., *supra* note 5, in light of the significant welfare losses.

and considering potential action. Indeed we can go further. In the case of social media, which I have emphasized here, many people face a Barbie Problem, which argues for policy reforms, perhaps above all to help young people against product traps. Private and public interventions, designed to help people to escape those traps, might increase social welfare; consider efforts to nudge teenagers not to spend time on social media platforms late at night. And if people are asked to waive their rights, it might be best to ban the waiver request. Waivers might well be Barbies.

The form of manipulation that I have been discussing here is quite general. If people can coordinate or make some kind of agreement, they might be able to find a way to protect themselves against harmful actions, including purchases of products that they wish did not exist. But coordination and agreement might not be possible. Sellers of various kinds count on that. This is a distinctive form of manipulation, and it ought to be addressed.

Part III
THE FUTURE

7 MANIPULATION-FREE NUDGING, 1

Every day, people are influenced without being manipulated. You might see a warning: "This product contains seafood." Or: "Smoking cause cancer." You might receive information: "Adults need 2,000 calories per day." You might receive a reminder: "Appointment for you at Internal Medicine on June 10, at 10:00 AM." Warnings, information, and reminders need not be manipulative. Or you might be automatically enrolled in something – say, green energy. Is that manipulative? As we have seen, the answer is not obvious.

Many people, including the present author, have been interested in "nudges," soon to be defined in more detail, and "choice architecture" as regulatory tools.[1] In Chapter 2, we saw that some nudges cross the line; they do count as forms of manipulation. The principal goal of this chapter, and the one that follows, is to explore whether and when nudges raise serious ethical problems. To make progress on that question, we will continue to explore manipulation, but we will be broadening the viewscreen to consider the ethical issues more generally.

As we shall see, those issues largely turn on whether nudges promote or instead undermine welfare, autonomy, and dignity. As we shall also see, the ethical analysis of nudges is similar to the corresponding analysis for other tools, such as fines and mandates.

---

[1] Some of the strongest objections can be found in Riccardo Rebonato, *Taking Liberties: A Critical Examination of Libertarian Paternalism* (2012).

But there are some distinctive wrinkles, involving potential threats to autonomy and dignity. In particular, a concern for personal agency often motivates the most plausible objections to nudges. Personal agency will therefore be a unifying theme here.

My central conclusion is that, at least if they are taken in general or in the abstract, the ethical objections lack much force, and for two different reasons. First, both nudges and choice architecture are inevitable, and it is therefore pointless to wish them away. Second, many nudges, and many forms of choice architecture, maintain and promote agency. They do not manipulate anyone. For example, disclosure of information ("this product contains seafood") need not be manipulative. Many nudges are defensible and may even be required on ethical grounds, whether we care about welfare, autonomy, dignity, or some other value.

It is true that all government action, including nudges, should face a burden of justification (and sometimes a heavy burden). If the government requires disclosure of information or automatically enrolls people in a health care plan, it must explain and defend itself. The fact that people retain freedom of choice, and are ultimately permitted to go their own way, is important, but it does not give public officials a license to do whatever they want. Manipulators do not remove freedom of choice. In many cases, however, the requisite explanation is available.

Suppose, for example, that we believe that the goal of social ordering (including those forms for which government is responsible) is to promote social welfare. If so, we will favor welfare-promoting nudges. Consider, for example, a disclosure requirement for credit card companies, designed to promote informed choices, and likely to achieve that goal. There is nothing manipulative or otherwise objectionable about that.

Or suppose that we believe in individual autonomy and dignity. If so, we will favor nudges and choice architecture that promote those values. Consider, for example, an effort to prompt people to make their own choices about what kind of retirement plan they want, by asking them precisely that question when they begin employment. That is not manipulative, though of course the question could be worded in a manipulative fashion. ("Yes! I want to take care of myself when I am older," or "No, I don't care at all about my future.")

If we value democratic self-government, we will be inclined to support nudges and choice architecture that do not manipulate people and that help to promote democratic goals. Any democracy has a form of choice architecture that helps define and constitute its own aspirations to self-government. Indeed, a Constitution can be seen as a kind of choice architecture for choice architects. A self-governing society might well nudge its citizens to participate in the political process and to vote. Political parties regularly engage in such nudging, and it is hardly illegitimate for public officials to encourage people to vote. In the United States, for example, some states have adopted a system of automatic voter registration, a form of choice architecture that is unambiguously designed to promote participation in the political process through exercise of the franchise.

Of course no one should approve of nudges or choice architecture in the abstract or as such. It remains possible that distrust of government, and faith in markets, will lead us to minimize nudging on welfarist or autonomy grounds. Some nudges, and some forms of choice architecture, do indeed run into convincing ethical objections, above all because they undermine welfare, autonomy, or dignity. They might be manipulative. As we saw in Chapter 2, relative risk information is a form of manipulation, and outcomes can be framed so as to manipulate people.

Nudges might also compromise rather than promote self-government. Suppose, for example, that a nation establishes a default rule stating that unless voters explicitly indicate otherwise, they will be presumed to support the incumbent leader in the election. Or suppose that a nation establishes a default rule to the effect that unless citizens indicate otherwise, their estates will revert to the nation's most powerful political party upon their death. There is ample reason to question a default rule of this kind even if citizens are authorized to opt out.

Some nudges have *illicit ends*, and they are objectionable for that reason. As we shall see, transparency and accountability are indispensable safeguards, and both nudges and choice architecture should be transparent. Even if so, there is a risk of manipulation, and that risk should be avoided.

I will be covering a great deal of territory, but three unifying themes should be kept in mind throughout. The first involves the relationship between nudges and human agency. When nudges are in place, human agency is retained (because freedom of choice is not removed), and agency always takes place in the context of some kind of choice architecture. This is not a sufficient justification for nudges, but it is important.

The second unifying theme involves the need to have a sufficiently capacious sense of the category of nudges, and a full appreciation of the differences among them. Some nudges are *educative*, but others are not; they are *architectural*. Some nudges enlist or combat behavioral biases, but others do not, and even among those that do enlist or combat such biases, there are significant differences. Many nudges are not even arguably manipulative; some can be taken to cross the line.

The third unifying theme is the need to bring ethical concerns in close contact with particular examples. A legitimate point about default rules may not apply to warnings or reminders. An ethical objection to the use of social norms may not apply to information disclosure. Here as elsewhere, abstraction can be a trap, and that will be one of my principal themes.

Concepts and Definitions

Nudges are interventions that steer people in particular directions but that also allow them to go their own way.[2] Because they maintain individual agency, they are liberty-preserving. A reminder is a nudge; so is a warning. A GPS device nudges; a warning light in your car nudges; so does a beeping sound, telling you that your car is getting close to another car. To qualify as a nudge, an intervention must not impose significant material incentives (including disincentives). A subsidy is not a nudge; a tax is not a nudge; a fine or a jail sentence is not a nudge.

To count as such, a nudge must fully maintain freedom of choice. If an intervention imposes significant material costs on choosers, it might, of course, be justified, but it is not a nudge. Some nudges work because they inform people; they are educative.

---

[2] *See* Richard H. Thaler and Cass R. Sunstein, *Nudge: Improving Decisions about Health, Wealth, and Happiness* 6 (2008) ("To count as a mere nudge, the intervention must be easy and *cheap to avoid*") (emphasis added).

Other nudges work because they make certain choices easier; for example, they might reduce sludge. Still other nudges work because of the power of inertia and procrastination.

When people make decisions, they do so against a background consisting of choice architecture. Have you been to an airport recently? You might notice that to get to the gate, the airport might be designed so that you pass a number of stores, or even have to walk through a store, step by step. I travel to Ireland frequently, and I much love Shannon Airport, which is convenient, fast, and simple. It's great! But if you are heading from Shannon to the United States, you will go through a large store, with all sorts of tempting items. I recently went through that store with my children and it was extremely difficult to get to the gate without making a few purchases. My kids were nudged. There's clever choice architecture there, and while it does not involve trickery, it could be characterized, not implausibly, as a form of manipulation (see definition (8) and also Barnhill's account, discussed in Chapter 1).

Any cafeteria has a design, and the design will affect what people choose. It can place healthy foods in a prominent position, or not. Department stores have architectures, and they can be designed so as to promote or discourage certain choices by shoppers (such as leaving without making a purchase). Even if the layout of a department store is a result of chance, or does not reflect the slightest effort to steer people, it will likely have consequences for what people end up selecting. If, for example, people see certain items first, they are more likely to buy them.[3] We have seen that certain forms of store design can plausibly be regarded as manipulative.

The same is true of websites. The best book on website design, I think, is called *Don't Make Me Think*, by Steve Krug.[4] The book is all about choice architecture and nudging, though it does not use the terms. Krug's first law of usability is captured in his title. A website, he urges, "should be self-evident. Obvious. Self-explanatory." He offers an assortment of principles designed to minimize cognitive effort on the part of users. He is an opponent

---

[3] Eran Dayan and Maya Bar-Hillel, Nudge to Nobesity II: Menu Positions Influence Food Orders, 6 *Judgment and Decision Making* 333 (2011).

[4] *See* Steve Krug, *Don't Make Me Think, Revisited: A Common Sense Approach to Web Usability* (3rd ed. 2013).

of sludge. He does not want users to have to ask questions. There is nothing manipulative about a website that is simple to use. A complex website, by contrast, might be designed so as to manipulate people.

Both private and public institutions (including courts) create default rules. In fact they cannot dispense without them. A cell phone, a mortgage, a tablet, and a welfare program will inevitably come with defaults, which can be changed if the relevant person or people agree. The law of contract is permeated with default rules, which establish what happens if people say nothing. People's legal relationships with their employer, their mortgage provider, their rental car company, their credit card company, and even their spouse and their children consist in large part of default rules. Consider, for example, implied warranties. If the contracting parties are silent on whether employment is terminable "at will" or "for cause," the law must supply a default; neither possibility is foreordained by nature or comes from the sky. Default rules nudge. They often operate like a GPS device, or even help to shape preferences and values.

To some people, this is a disturbing or even threatening fact. Insistent on individual agency, they are nervous about default rules. They are not at all enthusiastic about the idea that significant aspects of their lives are organized by such rules, which they did not themselves select, and which might well come from the practices, judgments, or wishes of other people. Nonetheless, that organization is in place. Moreover, it is true that some default rules are a product of traditions, customs, spontaneous orders, and invisible hands – a comfort to some people who especially distrust public officials. But it would be extravagant to say that all of them are. And even if they are, they will nudge individuals who live with them, and it takes real work to transform them into law, where they will have significant effects.

Even if a default rule is chosen on the ground that it captures what most people would do, and is in that sense "market-mimicking," it might well have some effect on preferences and outcomes. If people are defaulted into single-sided printing, they might grow to like single-sided printing. A default rule establishes people's initial entitlements (such as an entitlement to be fired only for cause), and it can be important for that reason, influencing people's preferences. For present purposes, the point is that default rules, of one or another kind, are sometimes unavoidable, or practically so.

We have also seen that attention is a scarce resource. When applications (for loans, for educational opportunities, for refinancing mortgages, for training, for financial benefits of any kind) are complex and difficult and full of sludge, people may not apply; a great deal of money might be lost as a result.[5] This point has implications for regulatory design. It suggests that the private sector may help or hurt people by focusing their attention in certain ways. The same is true for the public sector, whether or not it seeks to do so. A regulation might be written or applied in a way that makes certain features of a situation especially salient.

"Spontaneous orders" are celebrated by many people.[6] They are central to the liberal tradition. If an order is spontaneous, in the sense that it reflects the voluntary, bottom-up decisions of those who created it, there is some reason to think that it reflects the judgments of many people about how it makes best sense to proceed. On certain assumptions, spontaneous orders can promote people's welfare, but they are a form of choice architecture no less than intentional designs, and they will include a measure of nudging, not least if they create and perpetuate social norms (consider norms in favor of self-control and considerateness). Invisible hands can nudge every bit as much as the most visible ones. To be sure, spontaneous order and invisible hands may be less dangerous than intentional designs, and on certain (controversial) assumptions[7] they are likely to be benign (or better); but they are nonetheless forms of choice architecture. Are they manipulative? Usually not.

For the future, we could imagine new forms of choice architecture that are designed to improve anti-poverty programs; environmental programs; energy programs; retirement and social

---

[5] *See* Benjamin Keys et al., Failure to Refinance 1, 5 (NBER Working Paper No. 20798, 2014), www.nber.org/papers/w20401.
[6] *See* Friedrich Hayek, *Freedom, Reason, and Tradition* 229 (1958).
[7] Edna Ullmann-Margalit, The Invisible Hand and the Cunning of Reason, 64 *Social Research* 181 (1997), which shows the assumptions on which invisible hands might be reliable, and which questions those assumptions. For an extended exploration of why invisible hands might produce serious harm, *see* George Akerlof and Robert Shiller, *Phishing for Phools* (2015).

security programs; anti-obesity programs; educational programs; health care programs; and programs to increase organ donation. We could also imagine forms of choice architecture that are designed to combat race and sex discrimination, to help disabled people, and to promote economic growth. A great deal of future work needs to be devoted to choice architecture in these and related domains.

Still, there is no question that certain nudges, and certain kinds of choice architecture, can raise serious ethical problems. Consider, for example, a government that uses nudges to promote discrimination on the basis of race, sex, or religion. Any fascist government might well (and almost certainly does) nudge. Terrorists nudge. Even truthful information (for example, about crime rates) might fan the flames of violence and prejudice. (If people learn that bad behavior is widespread, they might be more likely to engage in that behavior, because it is the social norm.) Groups or nations that are committed to violence sometimes enlist nudges in their cause, often in the form of propaganda, which can in some forms be counted as a (bad) kind of nudge. And even if nudges do not have illicit ends, it is possible to wonder whether those who enlist them are treating people with respect.

The most prominent concerns about nudging and choice architecture point to three foundational commitments: welfare, autonomy, and dignity. Some nudges could run afoul of one or more of these commitments, perhaps because they are manipulative. It is easy to identify welfare-reducing nudges that lead people to waste time or money; an unhelpful default rule for health insurance could fall into that category, as could an educational campaign designed to persuade people to purchase excessive insurance or to make foolish investments. Nudges could be, and often are, harmful to the environment. Excessive pollution is, in part, a product of unhelpful choice architecture, because a wide range of default rules and legal permissions help make such pollution possible.

The Inevitability of Choice Architecture

Consider in this light a tale from the novelist David Foster Wallace: "There are these two young fish swimming along and they happen to meet an older fish swimming the other way, who nods at them and says 'Morning, boys. How's the water?' And the two young fish swim on for a bit, and then eventually one of them looks over at the other and goes 'What the hell is water?'"[8]

This is a tale about choice architecture. It is the equivalent of water. Weather is itself a form of choice architecture, because it influences what people decide.[9] Needless to say, human life is not imaginable without some kind of weather. Nature nudges. The common law is a regulatory system, and it will nudge, even if it allows people to have a great deal of flexibility.

In this light, choice architecture is inevitable. Human beings (or dogs, or cats, or horses) cannot wish it away. Any store has a design; some products are seen first, and others are not. Any menu places options at various locations. Television stations come with different numbers, and, strikingly, numbers can matter, even when the costs of switching are vanishingly low; people tend to choose the station at the lower number, so that Channel 3 will obtain more viewers than Channel 53.[10] Any website has a design, which will affect what and whether people will choose.[11]

Nor can the state avoid nudging. Suppose that a government is or purports to be firmly committed to free markets, private property, and laissez-faire. Even so, it cannot simply refrain from acting – or from nudging. It creates its own choice architecture. As Hayek wrote, the task of establishing a competitive system requires "indeed a wide and unquestioned field for state activity," for "in no system that could be rationally defended would the state just do nothing. An effective competitive system needs an intelligently designed and continuously adjusted legal framework as much as any other."[12]

As Hayek understood, a state that protects private property has to establish a set of prohibitions and permissions, including a set

---

[8] David Foster Wallace, In His Own Words, Intelligent Life (Sept. 19, 2008), https://fs.blog/david-foster-wallace-this-is-water/.
[9] *See* Meghan R. Busse et al., Projection Bias in the Car and Housing Markets 2 (NBER Working Paper No. 18212, 2014), www.nber.org/papers/w18212.
[10] *See* Gregory Martin and Ali Yurukoglu, Bias in Cable News: Real Effects and Polarization (NBER Working Paper No. 20798, 2014), www.nber.org/papers/w20798.
[11] Steve Krug, *Don't Make Me Think Revisited: A Common Sense Approach to Web and Mobile Usability* 10–19 (2014).
[12] F. A. Hayek, *The Road to Serfdom* 40 (1943).

of default entitlements, establishing who has what before bargaining begins. Recall that the rules of contract (as well as property and tort) provide a form of choice architecture for social ordering. I have noted that initial entitlements and default rules nudge because they affect people's preferences, even if transaction costs are low and people can bargain as they see fit. It remains true that choice architecture can maintain freedom of choice; it is also true that choice architects can at least aspire to neutrality along important dimensions. But choice architecture itself is inevitable, which means that it is pointless to object to it on ethical grounds.

Freedom

At the same time, we can imagine the following view: Some forms of choice architecture and nudging are unavoidable, to be sure, but it is important and good if they are the product of nature or some kind of spontaneous order, rather than of conscious design, or of the action of any designer. Perhaps the law can build on that order; perhaps the law of contract, property, and tort do exactly that. Invisible-hand mechanisms[13] often produce choice architecture. On a time-honored view, much of law is in fact "customary law." It codifies people's actual practices and it does not reflect any kind of dictation by public authorities. Consider Hayek's celebration of the "empiricist, evolutionary tradition," for which:

> [T]he value of freedom consists mainly in the opportunity it provides for the growth of the undesigned, and the beneficial functioning of a free society rests largely on the existence of such freely grown institutions. There probably never has existed a genuine belief in freedom, and there certainly has been no successful attempt to operate a free society, without a genuine reverence for grown institutions, for customs and habits . . .[14]

---

[13] For a superb discussion of invisible-hand explanations and their limitations, see Edna Ullmann-Margalit, Invisible-Hand Explanations, 39 *Synthese* 263 (1978).
[14] F. A. Hayek, *The Constitution of Liberty: The Definitive Edition* 122 (2013).

On this view, there is special reason, from the standpoint of freedom, for valuing forms of choice architecture that reflect the work of "grown institutions," rather than designed ones. We might be comfortable with any nudging that reflects "customs and habits," but suspicious of any nudging that displays no reverence for them. Here, then, is a foundation for skepticism about any kind of social engineering; the skepticism might be applied to nudges as well as to mandates and bans. We might be particularly concerned about government-designed choice architecture, on the ground that public officials lack the information or the incentives to be trusted.

Even if the law of contract, property, and tort constitute forms of choice architecture, and even if it is not quite customary (and involves a degree of dictation and design), the relevant architecture can be made as flexible as possible and maintain a great deal of room for private ordering – and thus for freedom. To summarize a lengthy argument:[15] The state, and the law, can provide the background rules for private interaction and decline to specify outcomes. Even if those rules turn out to nudge (as in the case of default rules), they are very different from social planning in all its forms – on one view, far more modest and less dangerous.

To be sure, the criminal law will include some dictation; no nation can deal with murder, assault, and rape with mere nudges. But perhaps the criminal law can restrict itself to prohibitions on force and fraud (and more generally play a role in correcting the standard market failures). A nation can certainly minimize the number of activities that it criminalizes. It might adopt a narrow account of the scope of the criminal law, perhaps focused on harm to others. And it might restrict any nudging to initiatives that operate in the service of the criminal law, narrowly conceived. For example, it might adopt public educational campaigns to discourage sexual violence.

On certain assumptions, much more in the way of self-conscious choice architecture by the state is especially worrisome, because it threatens welfare, autonomy, and dignity. But it is necessary to ask: What are those assumptions, and are they likely to be correct? Why and exactly when would spontaneous order be benign? (Is there some kind of social Darwinism behind enthusiasm

---

[15] *See generally* Friedrich Hayek, *The Constitution of Liberty* (1976).

for spontaneous order, reflecting a belief that voluntary choices and competition necessarily produce good results? That view is not easy to defend.) It is true that action by government poses dangers and risks, but efforts to defend spontaneous orders and invisible hands run into well-understood problems and objections, because there is no reason for confidence that the outcomes will be benign.

For example, a government that forbids discrimination on the basis of race and sex, or that takes steps to ensure reasonable accommodation of disabled people, is hardly relying on an invisible hand, and it is not drawing on custom. In any case, the argument for spontaneous orders seeks to restrict, above all, the coercive power of the state, not nudges as such. Whatever our theory of the legitimate domain of government, the most serious harms tend to come from mandates and bans (from genuine coercion), and not from nudges, which maintain freedom of choice.

It is true that spontaneous orders, invisible hands, and randomness can avoid some of the serious dangers, and some of the distinctive biases, that come from self-conscious nudging on the part of government. If we are especially fearful of official mistakes – coming from incompetence or bad motivations – we will want to minimize the occasions for nudging. And if we believe that invisible-hand mechanisms generally promote welfare or freedom, we will not want to disturb their products, even if those products include nudges.

In my view, however, the strong position in favor of spontaneous orders and invisible hands cannot be defended. But my goal here is not to justify that conclusion. The minimal point is that a degree of nudging by state officials cannot be avoided. If we are committed to spontaneous orders and invisible hands, we will be committed to a specific role for government, one that will include a specified choice architecture and specified nudges.

Abstraction Is a Trap

To come to terms with the ethical questions, it is important to bring first principles in contact with concrete practices. For purposes of orientation, it will be useful to give a more detailed accounting of actual and potential nudges. One reason is to avoid the trap of abstraction. As we shall see, the ethical evaluation of nudges depends on their concrete content, not on their status as nudges.

The most obvious nudges consist of default rules, which establish what happens if people do nothing at all. Others include sludge reduction and simplification (for example, of applications for building permits, job training, or financial aid); disclosure of factual information (for example, calorie labels); warnings, graphic or otherwise (for example, on cigarette packages); reminders (for example, of bills that are about to become due); increases in ease and convenience (for example, through website design); uses of social norms (for example, disclosure of how one's energy use compares to that of one's neighbors); nonmonetary rewards, such as public recognition; active choosing (as in the questions: *What retirement plan do you want?* or *Do you want to become an organ donor?*); and precommitment strategies (through which people agree, in advance, to a particular course of conduct, such as a smoking cessation program).

It is important to acknowledge that some nudges preserve freedom of choice for a relevant population, while mandating action from some other population. Suppose, for example, that the government requires large employers to adopt automatic enrollment plans for either retirement or for health insurance. If so, employees are nudged, but employers are coerced. Or suppose that the government requires chain restaurants (including movie theaters) to display calories to consumers. If so, customers are nudged, but restaurants are coerced. Some nudges from government take the form of requiring some group X to nudge some other group Y. This point should be kept in mind in evaluating ethical objections, because coercion raises distinctive concerns, and sometimes government coerces the private sector to nudge consumers.

Some nudges, imposed by regulatory agencies, attempt to counteract System 1 and to strengthen the hand of System 2 by improving the role of deliberation and people's considered judgments – as, for example, through disclosure of relevant information, debiasing,[16] and the use of precommitment strategies. Other nudges are designed to appeal to, or to activate, System 1 – as in the cases of graphic warnings. Some nudges do not appeal to System 1,

---

[16] *See generally* Christine Jolls and Cass R. Sunstein, Debiasing through Law, 35 J Legal Studies 199 (2006).

but work because of its operation – as, for example, where default rules have large effects because of the power of inertia.

A nudge might be justified on the ground that it helps counteract a behavioral bias, and (as we shall see) some people object to such efforts, especially if they seem to target or to exploit System 1. But (and this is an important point) a behavioral bias is *not* a necessary justification for a nudge, and nudges need not target or exploit System 1 in any way. Disclosure of information can be helpful even in the absence of any bias. A default rule simplifies life and might therefore be desirable whether or not a behavioral bias is involved. A GPS is useful even for people who do not suffer from a cognitive bias affecting their ability to drive to their desired destination.

As the GPS example suggests, many nudges have the goal of *increasing navigability* – of making it easier for people to get to their preferred destination. Such nudges stem from an understanding that life can be simple or hard to navigate, and a goal of helpful choice architecture is to promote simpler navigation. To date, there has been far too little attention to the close relationship between navigability and (good) nudges. Insofar as the goal is to promote navigability, the ethical objections are greatly weakened and might well dissipate.

Nudges can have a substantial effect on both individual lives and social welfare. In Denmark, for example, automatic enrollment in retirement plans has had a much larger effect than substantial tax incentives.[17] In the United States, efforts to inform consumers of how their energy use compares to that of their neighbors has had the same (significant) effect on household energy use as a significant spike in the short-term cost of electricity.[18] Simplification of the financial aid form, to assist people who seek to attend college, has been found to have as large an effect in promoting college attendance as a several thousand dollar increase in financial aid.[19]

---

[17] Raj Chetty et al., Active vs. Passive Decisions and Crowdout in Retirement Savings Accounts: Evidence from Denmark, 129 *Quarterly Journal of Economics* 1141 (2014).

[18] *See* Hunt Allcott, Social Norms and Energy Conservation, 95 *J Public Economics* 1082, 1082 (2011).

[19] *See* Eric Bettinger et al., The Role of Simplification and Information in College Decisions: Results from the H&R Block FAFSA Experience (NBER Working Paper No. 15361, 2009), www.nber.org/papers/w15361.

Varieties of Nudges

For purposes of evaluating the ethical questions, three distinctions are particularly important, because they help clarify the underlying concerns. First, *paternalistic nudges* should be distinguished from *market failure nudges*. Some of the most familiar nudges are designed to protect people from their own mistakes (including a behavioral bias); consider a default rule designed to increase savings. Other nudges are designed to respond to a standard kind of market failure, which can arise even if individuals are making no mistake at all (and so paternalism is not an issue). Consider a default rule designed to reduce pollution (as, for example, in the form of a default rule in favor of green energy).

In the category of market failure nudges, we can identify *externality-reducing nudges, prisoner's dilemma nudges*, and *coordination nudges*.[20] For nudges that fall into these categories, the governing question should be: Do they increase social welfare, rightly understood?[21] Cost-benefit analysis is the best available way of operationalizing that question, though it has significant gaps and limitations, not least if distributional considerations turn out to be relevant.

There is broad agreement that it is legitimate for government to respond to market failures. If the government is trying to reduce a collective action problem that produces high levels of pollution, it does not raise the kinds of ethical concerns that come into play if the government is acting paternalistically. It follows that market failure nudges should not be especially controversial in principle, though we might well worry over questions of effectiveness. In the face of a standard market failure, a mere nudge is usually not enough; coercion might well be justified (perhaps in the form of a corrective tax, perhaps in the form of a regulatory mandate). But a nudge might prove to be complementary to coercion, and, in some ways, it might be a substitute.

Second, *educative nudges* should be distinguished from nudges that *lack educative features, such as architectural nudges*.

---

[20] On coordination, with implications for productive nudges, *see* Edna Ullmann-Margalit, Coordination Norms and Social Choice, 11 *Erkenntnis* 143 (1977).

[21] Of course there is a great deal of dispute about how social welfare is rightly understood. For a valuable discussion, *see* Matthew D. Adler, *Well-Being and Fair Distribution* (2012).

Educative nudges attempt to inform people, so that they can make better choices for themselves. Other nudges, including architectural nudges, are meant to help people without necessarily increasing their knowledge or understanding; default rules have this characteristic. If the focus is on increasing people's own powers of agency, educative nudges should not be especially controversial on ethical grounds, and indeed they should be welcomed – though their benefits might not justify their costs, and though they can also run into problems of effectiveness.

Third, *nudges that enlist or exploit behavioral biases* should be distinguished from nudges that do no such thing. In particular, we have seen that some nudges enlist or exploit System 1 whereas other nudges appeal to System 2. Efforts to target, or to benefit from, behavioral biases tend to be more controversial, on ethical grounds, than efforts to appeal to deliberative capacities. The reason is that the former appear to be more manipulative and less respectful of people's capacity for agency (a point to which I will return).

It follows that the most controversial nudges are paternalistic, noneducative, and designed to enlist or exploit behavioral biases.

Illicit Reasons and Transparency

It must be acknowledged that choice architecture can be altered or that new nudges can be introduced for illicit reasons. Indeed many of the most powerful objections to nudges, and to changes in choice architecture, are based on a judgment that the underlying motivations are illicit. With these points, there is no objection to nudges as such; the objection is to the grounds for the particular nudges.

For example, an imaginable default rule might skew the democratic process by saying that voters are presumed to vote for the incumbent politician, unless they specify otherwise. Such a rule would violate principles of neutrality that are implicit in democratic norms; it would be unacceptable for that reason. Alternatively, a warning might try to frighten people by fabricating stories about the supposedly nefarious plans of members of a minority group. Social norms might be invoked to encourage people to buy unhealthy products ("most people are buying these products; you should too!"). In extreme cases, private or public institutions might try to nudge people toward violence.

It must also be acknowledged that the best choice architecture often calls for active choosing. Sometimes the right approach is to *require* people to choose, so as to ensure that their will is actually expressed. Sometimes it is best to *prompt* choice, by asking people what they want, without imposing any requirement that they do so. A prompt is emphatically a nudge, designed to get people to express their will, and it might be unaccompanied by any effort to steer people in a preferred direction – except in the direction of choosing.

Choice architecture should be transparent and subject to public scrutiny, certainly if public officials are responsible for it. At a minimum, this proposition means that when such officials institute some kind of reform, they must not hide it from the public. If officials issue a regulation changing a default rule so as to promote clean energy or conservation, they should disclose what they are doing, and they should also explain why they are doing it (with reference to any behavioral bias, if that is the reason for the change). Self-government itself requires public scrutiny of nudges. Such scrutiny is an important ex ante safeguard against harmful nudges; it is also an important ex post corrective. Transparency and public scrutiny can reduce the likelihood of welfare-reducing choice architecture. Nations should also treat their citizens with respect, and allowing public scrutiny shows a measure of respect – and simultaneously reduces the risk that nudges will reduce welfare, or intrude on autonomy or dignity.

There is a question whether transparency and public scrutiny are sufficient rather than merely necessary. The answer is that they are not sufficient. We could imagine forms of choice architecture that would be unacceptable even if they were fully transparent; consider (transparent) architecture designed to entrench inequality on the basis of sex. Here again, the problem is that the goals of the relevant nudge are illicit. As we shall see, it is also possible to imagine cases of manipulation in which the goals are not illicit, but in which the fact of transparency might not be sufficient to justify a nudge. A transparent nudge, announced in advance but taking the form of subliminal advertising of one or another kind, would run into legitimate objections about manipulation.

8 MANIPULATION-FREE NUDGING, 2

Let us now turn to nudges that are not designed to address a standard market failure and that are intended to help people to avoid their own mistakes. Such nudges ought not to be manipulative, but they might well be deemed paternalistic. A GPS device is not manipulative, but it is paternalistic; it instructs you to follow the route that it deems best for you, considering your goals. When third parties are not at risk, and when the welfare of choosers is all that is involved, the central objective of nudging is to "influence choices in a way that will make choosers better off, *as judged by themselves.*"[1] In many cases, that standard is straightforward to apply. If a GPS device steers people toward a destination that is not their own, it is not working well. And if it offers them a longer and less convenient route, it will not make choosers better off by their own lights (unless that is the route they want, perhaps because it is scenic).

Many nudges can be evaluated under the "as judged by themselves" standard; consider a reminder, a warning, a default rule, or disclosure of relevant information. To see whether the standard is met, we would have to take each nudge on its own. But the standard will often provide sufficient guidance.

So long as there is no manipulation, this understanding of the objective of nudging should go some way toward defusing the principal ethical concerns. If the choice architect is actually succeeding in making choosers better off by their own lights, there would

---

[1] Richard Thaler and Cass R. Sunstein, *Nudge: The Final Edition* 7 (2021).

seem to be no objection from the standpoint of welfare. Nor is it clear that there is a problem from the standpoint of autonomy or dignity. I will return to these points.

At the same time, it must be acknowledged that the standard runs into serious questions and challenges.

Objectively Good Lives

Some people believe that human lives can be objectively good or objectively bad, and that choosers can and do make objective mistakes about what makes their lives good. As they are understood in political philosophy, "perfectionist"[2] approaches emphasize the importance and legitimacy of increasing the likelihood that people will have lives that are actually good. A life that contains meaning, variety, and fulfillment might be thought to be objectively good; a life that is devoted to watching short videos on a cell phone might not be thought to fall in that category. (Of course there are different forms of perfectionism, and I am bracketing many complexities here.)

For people who embrace perfectionism, the "as judged by themselves" standard is based on a fundamental mistake, which is that it allows the subjective judgments of choosers to prevail even if they are objectively wrong. Imagine, for example, that a chooser makes decisions that ensure a life that is short and unhealthy, or that is without either meaning, variety, or pleasure, or that involves a great deal of suffering. It might be asked: Why should choice architects defer to choosers in such circumstances?

This question raises serious questions within political philosophy, which I cannot answer here.[3] To the extent that choice architects defer to choosers, it might be because of a moral judgment

---

[2] A form of liberal perfectionism is defended in Joseph Raz, *The Morality of Freedom* (1988). Perfectionism is criticized in Sarah Conly, *Against Autonomy* (2012), at 100–25.

[3] Relevant discussion can be found in Conly, *supra* note 2; B. Douglas Bernheim, The Good, the Bad, and the Ugly: A Unified Approach to Behavioral Welfare Economics, 71 *Journal of Benefit-Cost Analysis* 12 (2016); Martha Nussbaum, *Creating Capabilities* (2013); Amartya Sen, *Commodities and Capabilities* (1999). For a short, vivid set of objections to perfectionism, *see* Conly, *supra* note 2, at 109–25.

that choosers have ultimate sovereignty over their own lives, or it might be because of their own humility – their understanding that in general, and notwithstanding the existence of behavioral biases, they are likely have epistemic disadvantages as compared with those whose own lives are at stake. For present purposes, the central point is that insofar as choice architects adopt the "as judged by themselves" standard, they reject perfectionism, and they do so not inadvertently but on principle.

Before or After?

The "as judged by themselves" standard raises this question: Do we ask about choosers' judgments before the nudge, or instead after? Choosers' ex ante judgments might diverge from their ex post judgments. If choosers' judgments are influenced by the nudge, then *choice architects might be engineering the very judgment from which they are claiming authority.* That is a serious problem for the "as judged by themselves" standard.

Suppose, for example, that with a "green" default rule – one that provides an environmentally friendly energy provider, subject to opt out in favor of a cheaper but environmentally inferior provider – choosers (or a majority) are perfectly content. But suppose that they (or a majority) would also be content with the opposite default rule. Which judgments matter? Wherever the nudge influences choosers' judgments, that question raises serious puzzles.

In some cases, the nudge is unlikely to affect choosers' judgments; they will be the same ex ante and ex post. Whatever the default rule, most people are not likely to want to devote 50 percent of their salary to savings, or to have a health insurance policy that does not pay for surgeries, or to have meals that consist of old salami slices on stale bread. But when ex post and ex ante judgments differ, the standard becomes more difficult to apply. One option would be to use active choosing to see what people actually want. Another would be to explore the number of opt-outs under different default rules.[4] A third would be to attempt a more direct inquiry into

---

[4] Thaler and Sunstein, *supra* note 1.

people's welfare under different forms of choice architecture, though admittedly any such inquiry raises challenges of its own.

Preferences about Preferences

A separate question is raised by the fact that people do not only have preferences (or first-order preferences); they also have preferences about their preferences (or second-order preferences).[5] People might want to eat delicious but fattening foods, or to spend most of their monthly salary every month, but they might not want to want those things. In applying the "as judged by themselves standard," should choice architects consult first-order or second-order preferences?

Some imaginable cases are difficult, but in general the answer is straightforward: If second-order preferences reflect System 2 thinking – understood, in this context, as people's reflective judgments as opposed to their momentary impulses – there is a strong argument that such preferences have authority.[6] To be sure, System 1 has its claims. If people greatly enjoy certain activities, their enjoyment should not be disparaged; it is part of what makes life worth living. If a nudge discourages people from eating foods that they enjoy, or from engaging in activities that they love, it is imposing a genuine welfare loss. But if people think, on reflection, that the nudge is directing them in a way that they endorse, then the "as judged by themselves" standard is met.[7]

When we ask about choosers' judgments, what kind of information do we expect choosers to have? It makes sense to say

---

[5] *See* Harry Frankfurt, Freedom of the Will and the Concept of a Person, 68 *J of Philosophy* 5 (1971).
[6] I am bracketing some complexities here. For example, people's intuitions might be well trained, and their reflective judgments might be unreliable. We could imagine a tennis player who knows exactly what to do when a first serve goes to his backhand, even though he would not do very well in giving a reflective explanation, to himself or to others, what to do in those circumstances.
[7] There are, however, some difficult questions raised by time inconsistency. Suppose that at Time 1, Edward wants to engage in some behavior, and does, and enjoys a welfare gain, but at Time 2, Edward wishes that his former self had not engaged in that behavior, and experiences a welfare loss. If so, "as judged by themselves" standard runs into genuine challenges. *See* Douglas Whitman and Mario Rizzo, The Problematic Welfare Standards of Behavioral Paternalism, 6(3) *Review of Philosophy & Psychology* 409–25 (2015).

that choice architects should defer to choosers' informed judgments, rather than their uninformed ones. But if choice architects do not focus on choosers' actual judgments, and instead ask what choosers would do if they were informed, there is a risk that choice architects will be relying on their own values and beliefs, rather than choosers' own. In any case, such architects might lack sufficient information to know whether informed choosers deem themselves to be better off. It might not be at all simple for outsiders to compare (from the point of view of informed choosers) the various outcomes that stem from different nudges.

In some cases, these points might raise serious conceptual and empirical challenges. Nonetheless, the idea of choosers' informed judgments serves as the lodestar, and it imposes real discipline. Certainly choice architects should be focused on the welfare of choosers, rather than their own.

There are also hard questions about how to handle the "as judged by themselves" standard in the face of self-control problems. Suppose that someone faces such problems and is aware of that fact – but nonetheless wishes, at Time 1, to give into his impulses. Do we look to the assessment of (1) the alcoholic, who really wants that beer; (2) the would-be former alcoholic, who wants to quit; or (3) the actual former alcoholic, who is grateful to have been nudged away from alcoholism? In some ways, this question replicates those involving ex ante versus ex post judgments, and also those involving preferences about preferences. But insofar as the focus is on self-control problems, the issue is distinctive.

It is reasonable to insist that most former alcoholics are glad that they are no longer alcoholics (at least in the absence of highly unusual circumstances). For that reason, there is a strong argument that the "as judged by themselves" criterion should be taken to refer to the judgment of the person who is no longer in the grip of an addiction. That proposition is sufficient to resolve many real-world cases. Nonetheless, there can be a thin line between a self-control problem and a legitimate focus on short-term pleasure; that question deserves more extended treatment. No choice architect should engage in a program of nudging that disregards the importance of short-term pleasures, or pleasures in general, which are, of course, crucial parts of good lives.

Applied Ethics

I have suggested that the principal ethical objections to nudges point to welfare, autonomy, and dignity. I now turn to those objections. I shall also offer a few words about the risk of ignorant or biased choice architects.

Choice architecture may or may not be paternalistic. But it is true that nudges can be seen as a form of libertarian paternalism insofar as they attempt to use choice architecture to steer choosers in directions that will promote their welfare (again, as judged by choosers themselves). If we believe that choosers know best, any such effort at steering might seem misguided, at least if autonomy or welfare is our lodestar.

To evaluate this objection, it is important to see that we are speaking here of a distinctive form of paternalism in the sense that it is at once (a) soft and (b) means-oriented. It is soft insofar as it avoids coercion or material incentives and thus fully maintains freedom of choice. It is means-oriented insofar as it does not attempt to question or alter people's ends. Like a GPS device, it respects those ends (subject to the various complexities discussed above). It helps people to get where they want to go. To those who object to paternalism on welfare grounds, the most serious concerns arise in the face of manipulation or coercion (where freedom of choice is blocked) and when social planners, or choice architects, do not respect people's ends. To this extent, nudges aspire to avoid some of the standard welfarist objections to paternalism.

Nonetheless, some skeptics, concerned about welfare, object to paternalism as such.[8] Perhaps people are the best judges not only of their ends, but also of the best means to achieve those ends, given their own tastes and values. (People might reject the route suggested by the GPS on the ground that they prefer the scenic alternative; the GPS might not easily capture or serve their ends.) Moreover, the distinction between means and ends is not always simple and straightforward. One question is the level of abstraction at which

---

[8] *See*, e.g., Riccardo Rebonato, *Taking Liberties: A Critical Examination of Libertarian Paternalism* (2012).; Joshua D. Wright and Douglas H. Ginsburg, Behavioral Law and Economics: Its Origins, Fatal Flaws, and Implications for Liberty, 106 *Nw U Law Review* 1033 (2012).

we describe people's ends. If we describe people's ends at a level of great specificity – eating that brownie, having that cigarette, texting while driving – then people's means effectively *are* their ends. The brownie is exactly what they want; it is not a means to anything at all (except the experience of eating it).

If, by contrast, we describe people's ends at a level of high abstraction – "having a good life" – then nearly everything is a means to those ends. But if we do that, then we will not be capturing people's actual concerns; we will be disregarding what matters to them. These points do raise some problems for those who favor a solely means-oriented form of paternalism. They must be careful to ensure that they are not describing people's ends at a sufficiently high level of abstraction as to misconceive what people care about.

But insofar as a GPS device is a guiding analogy, it is not easy to see nudges as objectionable on welfare grounds. Many nudges are entirely focused on helping people to identify the best means for achieving their own preferred ends. Consider cases in which people are *mistaken about facts* (with respect to the characteristics of, say, a consumer product or an investment). If a nudge informs them, then it is respecting their ends and is likely to promote their welfare. Or suppose that certain product characteristics are in some sense shrouded, and the nudge helps people to see them for what they are. Or suppose that people suffer from a behavioral bias – perhaps because they are present-biased, perhaps because of unrealistic optimism. A nudge that corrects their mistake can help them to achieve their own ends.

To be sure, some behavioral biases are not so easy to analyze in these terms. If people suffer from present bias, is a nudge a form of paternalism about means? Suppose that people eat high-calorie food, or drink a great deal, or fail to exercise, because they value today and tomorrow, and not so much next year or next decade. If a nudge succeeds in getting people to focus on their long-term interests, it might increase aggregate (intrapersonal) welfare over time. But is such a nudge focused solely on means? If a person is seen as a series of selves extending over time, the choice architect is effectively redistributing welfare from earlier selves to later ones (and possibly maximizing people's lifetime welfare as well). But it is not entirely clear that we can speak, in such cases, of means paternalism. And if a person is seen as continuous over time, and not a series of selves, efforts to counteract present bias are, by hypothesis, undermining the ends of the chooser at the time of choice.

A principal reason for regulators and other policymakers to reject any form of paternalism involves welfare: Perhaps people are the best judges of what will promote their interests, and perhaps outsiders will blunder (as John Stuart Mill believed[9]). Recall Hayek's suggestion that "the awareness of our irremediable ignorance of most of what is known to somebody [who is a chooser] is *the chief basis of the argument for liberty.*"[10] A form of paternalism that maintains freedom of choice, and that is focused on means, is less likely to be objectionable on welfare grounds, certainly if we attend to behavioral biases.

In fact it is even possible that welfarists should ultimately embrace coercive paternalism, at least in the face of such biases.[11] When paternalism would improve welfare, welfarists should support paternalism. For welfarists, paternalism should be evaluated on a case-by-case basis – unless there is some systematic reason to support a presumption against paternalism.

Perhaps there is good reason for such a presumption, rooted in a judgment that choosers are likely to have better information than choice architects.[12] But in some cases, that judgment is incorrect, because choosers lack knowledge of facts. Educative nudges are a natural corrective. In some cases, a good default rule – say, automatic enrollment in pension programs – is hard to reject on welfarist grounds.

To be sure, active choosing might be better than a default rule, but that conclusion is not obvious; active choosing might impose real burdens on choosers (who would prefer not to choose) and might not reduce errors.[13] Welfarists might well be inclined to favor choice-preserving approaches, on the theory that individuals

---

[9] John Stuart Mill, *On Liberty* 8 (1859) (Kathy Casey ed. 2002).
[10] Friedrich Hayek, The Market and Other Orders, *in The Collected Works of F.A. Hayek* 384 (Bruce Caldwell ed. 2013) (emphasis added).
[11] Conly, *supra* note 2, at 32.
[12] See ibid. at 211. For another, nonwelfarist view of what is wrong with paternalism, see Nicholas Cornell, A Third Theory of Paternalism, 113 *Michigan Law Review* 1295 (2015) (arguing that paternalism may be wrong because it implies, and expresses a judgment, that the chooser is incapable of making good choices for herself).
[13] *See* Cass R. Sunstein, *Choosing Not to Choose: Understanding the Value of Choice*, 144–9 (2015).

usually well know what best fits their circumstances, but if welfare is our guide, the fact that a default rule has a paternalistic dimension should not be decisive against it.

A Muscle

Consider here a different kind of concern, one that also grows from a focus on welfare: *Choice-making is a muscle, and the ability to choose well can be strengthened through exercise.* If nudges would make the muscle atrophy, we would have an argument against them, because people's welfare depends on muscle-strengthening. We could imagine an ethical objection that would contend that some nudges do not allow people to build up their own capacities, and might even undermine their incentive to do so. If so, people's welfare is reduced (and it should be easy to see that there is an autonomy concern as well).

Here too, it is necessary to investigate the particulars – the kinds of nudges and choice architecture that are involved. Active choosing and prompted choice hardly impede learning. Nor do information and reminders. On the contrary, they promote learning. Nudges of this kind exercise the choice-making muscle, rather than the opposite. At least this is so if they are not manipulative.

With respect to learning, a potential problem does come from default rules. It is possible to say that active choosing is far better than defaults, simply because choosing may promote learning. Consider, for example, the question whether employers should ask employees to make active choices about their retirement plans, or whether they should instead default people into plans that fit their situations. The potential for learning might well count in favor of active choosing; if employees must choose, and if they are helped or encouraged to learn, the resulting knowledge might stand them in good stead for the rest of their lives. If people are defaulted into certain outcomes, they do not add to their stock of knowledge, and that may be a significant lost opportunity.

But the argument for learning depends on the setting. (Recall the earlier discussion of educative nudges.) There are domains in which the choice-making muscle needs rest rather than exercise. For most people, it is not important to become experts in the numerous decisions that lead to default settings in cell phones, and hence the use of such settings is not objectionable. The same point holds in many other contexts in which institutions rely on defaults rather than active choosing. Retirement saving might itself be such a context. To know whether choice architects should opt for active choosing, it is necessary to explore whether the context is one in which it is valuable, all things considered, for choosers to acquire a stock of knowledge. It is not necessarily terrible if employers create default allocations for retirement plans, so long as those allocations are in the interest of all or most employees.

It is true, of course, that education well might be the appropriate response if people are likely to make mistakes (whether they lack information or suffer from some kind of behavioral bias). Much of the time, the first and the best line of defense is education, which might itself be characterized as a nudge, and which certainly counts as a form of choice architecture. Some people, above all the psychologist Ralph Herwig, have written in favor of "boosts," designed to improve people's capacities; boosts might be preferred to nudges. We have seen that educative nudges are an important part of the repertoire of the choice architect. Invoking this point, Jeremy Waldron writes: "I wish, though, that I could be made a better chooser rather than having someone on high take advantage (even for my own benefit) of my current thoughtlessness and my shabby intuitions."[14]

Fair enough, but boosts and education have their limits. People benefit from default rules with respect to cell phones, tablets, health insurance policies, and rental car agreements. If people had to obtain sufficient education on all of the underlying issues, they would quickly run out of time. Simplification is often a blessing. On welfare grounds, a default rule is often the best approach, because it would preserve desirable outcomes (again, from the standpoint of choosers themselves) without requiring people to take the functional equivalent of a course in, say, statistics or finance.

For the welfarist, there is a recurring question whether, in particular circumstances, the costs of education justify the benefits. For those who are engaged in many activities, it would be impossibly

---

[14] *See* Jeremy Waldron, It's All For Your Own Good, *New York Review of Books* (2014), www.nybooks.com/articles/archives/2014/oct/09/cass-sunstein-its-all-your-own-good/. On boosts, see Ralph Hertwig, When to Consider Boosting: Some Rules for Policy-makers, 1 *Behavioral Public Policy* 143 (2017).

demanding to insist on the kind of education that would allow active choices about all relevant features. Default rules may well be best. Everything depends on the facts, but if welfare is our guide, there is a good argument that default rules are preferable to financial education with respect to important retirement issues.

Autonomy

Let us now switch from welfare and return to one of our general themes: An independent reason to reject paternalism involves autonomy and the idea of respect for persons. Stephen Darwall writes that the:

> [O]bjectionable character of paternalism of this sort is not that those who seek to benefit us against our wishes are likely to be wrong about what really benefits us .... It is, rather, primarily a failure of respect, a failure to recognize the authority that persons have to demand, within certain limits, that they be allowed to make their own choices for themselves.[15]

Fair enough. Do nudges intrude on autonomy? The answer depends on what kind of nudge is involved. Many nudges promote autonomy. A choice should not be considered autonomous if it is based on ignorance; if someone takes a stomach medicine in the belief that it will help with a cold, there is no interference with autonomy in informing him that it is stomach medicine. Autonomy requires informed choices, and educative nudges are designed specifically to ensure that choices are informed.

In the face of a behavioral bias, or some kind of systematic mistake (by the actor's own lights), it is hardly clear that a nudge infringes on autonomy, rightly understood.[16] When nudges help

---

[15] See Stephen Darwall, The Value of Autonomy and the Autonomy of the Will, 116 Ethics 263, 268 (2006).
[16] See Conly, *supra* note 2, at 36 ("Even if we accept that individuals have rights, and thus claims not to be harmed by others in certain ways, or to have (yet) others defend them in these claims, why would there be such a right here, where the point of the action is to help the person achieve what in the long run, he wants, and what he would want not if he were not a flawed thinker?").

correct some kind of bias, they might well promote people's autonomy – most obviously when they help people to have a better understanding of the facts. Suppose that because of the availability heuristic, people are far more fearful of some infectious disease (say, Ebola) than statistical reality warrants, and that a nudge gives them a more accurate sense of the risk of getting the disease. Many nudges promote people's capacity for agency; they do not undermine it. A nudge may promote autonomy if it counteracts present bias or unrealistic optimism, or allows people to see aspects of situations that would otherwise be shrouded or invisible. As we have seen, some people are troubled by the potential tension between government nudges and individual agency. But for educative nudges, there is no such tension; because of nudges, agency is actually increased.

It is also important to see that autonomy does not require choices everywhere. It does not justify an insistence on active choosing in all contexts. If we had to make choices about everything that affects us, we would quickly be overwhelmed. There is a close relationship between time-management and autonomy. People should be allowed to devote attention to the questions that, in their view, deserve their attention. If people have to make choices everywhere, their autonomy is reduced, if only because they cannot focus on those activities that seem to them most worthy of their attention.[17] Architectural nudges can promote autonomy in this light. They give people more control over the fabric of their own lives. Examples include automatic enrollment in health care and retirement plans.

It is nonetheless true that on grounds of autonomy (as well as welfare), the best choice architecture often calls for active choosing. Even though default rules preserve freedom of choice, they might intrude on autonomy, at least if they do not track people's likely choices. The problem is that because of the force of inertia, people might not reject harmful defaults. If so, there is arguably an intrusion on people's autonomy because they will end up with outcomes that they do not like and did not specifically select. Consider, for example, a default rule that says that if you do not

---

[17] *See* Sendhil Mullainathan and Eldar Shafir, *Scarcity* (2013), at 41.

indicate otherwise, you are presumed to be a member of a political party that you deplore, or to want your estate to go to the Vatican. Even though people can opt out, default rules can intrude on autonomy insofar as they impose that burden on people – and insofar as the particular rules (a) might stick because of that very burden and (b) do not reflect what informed people would like.

To return to one of my general themes: Whether the interest in autonomy calls for active choosing, as opposed to reliance on a default rule, depends on the circumstances. Manipulation should be off-limits; a central reason is that it violates autonomy. Along some dimensions, default rules are actually superior to active choosing on autonomy grounds. If people choose not to choose, or if they would make that choice if asked, it is an insult to their autonomy to force them to choose. And if people would like to choose, a default rule does not deprive them of that choice; they can reject the default. Even in the face of inertia, many people will do so. Preservation of freedom of choice is not sufficient, but so long as manipulation is not involved, it goes some distance toward ensuring that people's autonomy is respected. The same can be said for a requirement that any paternalistic nudges focus on people's own ends and otherwise have legitimate goals. But with respect to autonomy, a continuing problem lies in the possibility of manipulation (on which more in Chapter 9).

Insofar as nudges respect freedom of choice, they are, along an important dimension, preserving people's autonomy. Once choice architects coerce people, they are no longer merely nudging. But if they are focused on autonomy, skeptics might again argue that the problems associated with coercion cannot be entirely avoided with some nudges. We have seen that because of the power of inertia, people might accept (passively) a default rule even though they have no enthusiasm for the outcome that it produces, and would reject that outcome if they focused on the issue involved. Default rules can turn out to be manipulative (see Chapter 2).

We should doubt whether such situations are properly described as involving coercion. No one is being forced to do anything. But there is certainly a risk that a default rule will produce harmful results. Choice architects need to take account of that risk and take steps to ensure that freedom of choice is maintained and real. So long as it is, coercion is not involved.

Dignity

The idea of "dignity" is complex and contested.[18] On one view, autonomy and dignity are closely related. But in both politics and law, dignity sometimes occupies a distinctive place. In German constitutional law, for example, dignity has a prominent role, with the Constitution starting with these words: "Human dignity is inviolable [*unantastbar*]. To respect it and protect it is the duty of all state power."

We might begin by suggesting that the antonym of autonomy is coercion; the antonym of dignity is humiliation.[19] As I understand it here, the idea of dignity requires respect for people as agents; a person's dignity is not respected if he is treated as an infant or a thing, subject to the superior authority of another. A noncoercive intervention, respectful of people's autonomy, might nonetheless compromise dignity. Manipulation can do that. We have seen that if a doctor frames a choice in a certain way ("with this medicine, you can cut your risk in half"), he might be manipulating you, because the frame makes it difficult to make a reflective and deliberative choice. (Suppose that you face a risk of two in a million, and the medicine will reduce your risk to one in a million.) Or imagine, for example, that an employer allows employees a great deal of room for free choice but speaks to them as if they are children who have difficulty in engaging in even minimal forms of reasoning. A police officer can also fail to treat citizens with dignity even if he respects their autonomy (though again, we could understand autonomy in a way that is coextensive with dignity). A police officer can manipulate citizens and thus violate their autonomy.

Some nudges might seem to compromise dignity and respect for persons. They might humiliate people. As we shall see, this objection is both interesting and important, especially when it is combined with a concern about manipulation. Imaginable forms of choice architecture could indeed undermine dignity.

---

[18] For an especially valuable discussion, *see* Michael Rosen, *Dignity: Its History and Meaning* (2012). In the legal context, *see* Christopher McCrudden, Human Dignity and Judicial Interpretation of Human Rights, 19 *European J International Law* 655 (2008).

[19] *See* Avishai Margalit, *The Decent Society* 9–27 (1998).

There are, of course, large questions about the place of dignity in ethics.[20] On one (admittedly unconventional) view, dignity is properly part of an assessment of welfare. If people feel humiliated, or think that they have been treated disrespectfully, they suffer a welfare loss. That loss might be extremely serious. In any assessment of welfare consequences, such a loss must be considered. It might turn out to be exceedingly important, and to argue against particular nudges.

To avoid obtuseness, a good welfarist should acknowledge that an offense to dignity is qualitatively distinct. In its very nature, it is a different kind of loss from the loss of, say, money, or an opportunity to visit a beach. But on the welfarist view, a dignity loss is just one kind of welfare loss, to be weighed against the other goods that are at stake. Suppose, for purposes of argument, that a graphic and highly emotional appeal, triggering strong, System 1 emotions in order to discourage people from smoking, is plausibly seen as an offense to dignity – as a way of treating smokers disrespectfully (and perhaps infantilizing them). Some smokers might so regard such an appeal and object for that reason. But a welfarist might be willing to support the emotional appeal, notwithstanding the relevant loss, if it saves a significant number of lives.

On a different view, an insult to dignity is not merely part of a welfarist calculus. Such an insult does not depend on people's subjective feelings, and it is a grave act, perhaps especially if it comes from government. An insult to dignity, understood as a failure to treat people with respect, should not be permitted unless it has an overwhelmingly strong justification. If we endorse this view, it is especially important to ask whether nudges offend human dignity.

To return to my general plea: The force of the objection depends on the particular nudge. A GPS device insults no one's dignity. Disclosure of factual information can hardly be seen as an offense to dignity – certainly if the information is useful and not based on a false and demeaning belief that people need it. But we can

---

[20] See ibid.; see generally Rosen, supra note 18; Charles Beitz, Human Dignity in the Theory of Human Rights, 41 *Philosophy & Public Affairs* 259 (2013); Thomas Christiano, *Two Conceptions of Human Dignity as Persons* (2008) (unpublished manuscript).

easily imagine nudges that would offend one or another conception of dignity, perhaps because they are manipulative. Consider a public health campaign, directed at the prevention of obesity, that stigmatizes and humiliates people who are overweight by portraying them in a demeaning light. Or consider an antismoking campaign that did the same for smokers.

Here again, the fact that nudges preserve freedom of choice, and do not require anyone to do anything, should not be taken as a license to do anything at all. It is possible to imagine public education campaigns that are manipulative and that do offend dignity, and some real-world campaigns might suffer from that vice.

It might also count as an insult to dignity, and a form of infantilization, if the government constantly reminds people of things that they already know. Every child, and everyone who was once a child, can recall this form of infantilization, and it is not always absent from adult life as well. If people are informed of the same thing every hour or even every day (say, by their spouse, by their doctor, or by some public official), they might legitimately feel that their dignity is not being respected.

At the same time, most reminders, warnings, and uses of social norms do not demean anyone. Nor are choice architects likely to be humiliating choosers if they spread information about what most people do. In some cases, however, the concern about dignity might become more serious. If people are frequently reminded that a due date is coming, they might feel as if they are being treated like children. Warnings can run into the same concern insofar as they are repetitive or condescending, or are meant to trigger strong emotions instead of merely giving people a sense of factual realities. In some cases, warnings can be manipulative.

Here as well, there is no objection to the relevant nudges in the abstract, but there could well be concerns about specific types of nudges. At the same time, it must be emphasized that the relevant offense to dignity – coming from unwelcome and numerous reminders or warnings – is relatively minor, and from the standpoint of the concerns that have produced the focus on dignity in the Western political tradition, it is laughably modest.

What is the relationship between dignity and default rules? If an employer automatically enrolls employees into retirement and health care plans, dignity is hardly at risk. If a cell phone company adopts a series of default rules for the phone and the contractual arrangement, nothing need be amiss in terms of dignity. But we could imagine harder cases. Suppose that the government insisted on "default meals" in various restaurants so that people would be given certain healthy choices unless they specifically chose otherwise. Put to one side the fact that with respect to restaurants, this approach is a mandate, not a mere nudge. A plausible response is based on a concern about dignity: Why require default meals? Why shouldn't free people simply be asked to select what they want? Or suppose that a government specified a "default exercise plan" for adults, so that they would be presumed to want to engage in certain activities unless they opted out. People might offer the same plausible response, perhaps with considerable agitation.

Note that default rules of this kind might be objectionable for both welfarists and nonwelfarists. Welfarists might want to focus on people's subjective feelings. If people believe that they are being treated as children, and if they object to that treatment, welfarists should count this objection in their assessment of costs and benefits. Nonwelfarists would insist that the offense to dignity is objectionable even if it has some kind of welfarist justification.

In extreme situations, default rules could indeed be a serious affront to dignity. If so, there should be a strong presumption against them (whatever our foundational commitments). But (one more time) it would be a mistake to use extreme situations or barely imaginable cases as a reason to challenge default rules in general. People are not treated disrespectfully if an institution adopts a double-sided default for printing or if they are automatically enrolled in health insurance or retirement plans. The objection from dignity has far more force in the abstract than in the context of all, or nearly all, real-world cases in which default rules are actually at work.

Biased Officials

Choice architects are emphatically human, and fully subject to behavioral biases; they are often unreliable. The growing field of behavioral public choice draws on this point to offer an account of official error.[21] It is reasonable to object to some nudges, and to some efforts to intervene in existing choice architecture, on the ground that the choice architects might blunder. They might lack important information (the knowledge problem). They might be biased, perhaps because their own parochial interests are at stake (the public choice problem). They might themselves display behavioral biases – such as present bias, optimistic bias, or probability neglect. In a democratic society, public officials are responsive to public opinion, and if the public is mistaken, officials might be mistaken as well.

It is unclear whether and to what extent this objection is a distinctly ethical one, but it does identify an important cautionary note. One reason for nudges, as opposed to mandates and bans, is that choice architects may err. No one should deny that proposition, which argues strongly in favor of choice-preserving approaches. If choice architects blunder, at least it can be said that people are entitled to go their own way. And if we emphasize the risk of official error, we might want to avoid nudges and choice architecture as well.

The initial response to this objection should be familiar: Choice architecture is inevitable. When choice architects act, they alter the architecture; they do not create an architecture where it did not exist before. A certain degree of nudging from the public sector cannot be avoided, and there is no use in wishing it away. Nonetheless, choice architects who work for government might decide that it is best to try to rely on free markets and to trust free markets and invisible-hand mechanisms. If so, they would select (or accept) choice architecture that reflects those mechanisms.

This idea raises many conceptual and empirical puzzles, to which I have referred above, and which I will not engage in further detail here. The question is whether it is so abstract, and so rooted in dogmas, that it ought not to command support. To be sure, free markets have virtues. But in some cases, disclosure, warnings, and reminders can do far more good than harm. As we have seen, active

---

[21] For one example, see Timur Kuran and Cass R. Sunstein, Availability Cascades and Risk Regulation, 51 *Stanford Law Review* 683 (1999). For an overview, see Jan Schnellenbach and Christian Schubert, Behavioral Public Choice: A Survey (2014), http://papers.ssrn.com/sol3/papers.cfm?abstract_id=2390290.

choosing is sometimes inferior to default rules. Someone has to decide in favor of one or another, and in some cases, that someone is inevitably the government. It is true that distrust of public officials might argue against nudging, at least where it is avoidable, but if it is dogmatic and generalized, such distrust will likely produce serious losses in terms of welfare, autonomy, and even dignity. Invisible hands can and do compromise all of those things.

Agency as a Master Value

It is pointless to object to nudges and choice architecture as such. Human beings cannot live in a world without them. Spontaneous orders and invisible hands have many virtues, but they nudge. Even the most minimal government must create choice architecture of many different kinds. The common law itself influences people's decisions whether or not it was designed to do so (or designed at all). Return to the effects of default rules, of the sort that are pervasive in the law of property, contract, and tort.

Many nudges, and many changes in choice architecture, are not merely permissible on ethical grounds; they are actually required. On grounds of welfare, the point should be straightforward; much nudging promises to increase social welfare. But the point holds for autonomy and dignity as well. In some cases, there is an imaginable tension between nudges and human agency. But whether nudges compromise agency depends on their content, not their status as nudges. As we have seen, many nudges promote agency.

It is important to have a sufficiently capacious sense of the category of nudges, and a full appreciation of the differences among them. To make progress, ethical concerns must be brought into close contact with particular examples. It is true that any alterations in choice architecture, including those that preserve freedom, can run into serious and even convincing ethical objections – most obviously, where the underlying goals are illicit. But where the goals are legitimate, nudges are less likely to run afoul of ethical constraints, not least when they promote informed choices (as in the case of reminders). Transparency and public scrutiny are important safeguards, especially when public officials are responsible for nudges and choice architecture. Nothing should be hidden or covert.

The history of freedom-respecting nations is full of changes in choice architecture that have been motivated by an aspiration to realize the highest and most enduring of national ideals. In moving closer to those ideals, new nudges, increasing individual agency, will prove indispensable.

9 ARTIFICIAL INTELLIGENCE: PROMISE AND THREAT

Stories of a dystopian future often depict two different forms of human slavery. The first invokes the fear of pain; the second points to the appeal of pleasure. Manipulators have a field day with both pain and pleasure.

In the twentieth century, the two forms of slavery were defined, respectively, by George Orwell's *Nineteen Eighty-Four* and Aldous Huxley's *Brave New World*. Orwell's book is a nightmare of a totalitarian state, in which Big Brother rules by terror, and in which everyone is potentially vulnerable to official imprisonment or torture. Because Big Brothers can be found all over the world, and because of its searing account of how free will might be broken ("He loved Big Brother"), Orwell's tale has enduring resonance.

In Orwell's world, imprisonment and terror are accompanied by a great deal of manipulation. Consider this: "Power is in tearing human minds to pieces and putting them together again in new shapes of your own choosing." Or this: "It's a beautiful thing, the destruction of words." Or this, above all: "We do not merely destroy our enemies; we change them."[1]

By contrast, Huxley's book is a nightmare of consumerism, in which people are enslaved by their desire for pleasure, provided above all by the fictitious drug "soma." In Huxley's world, people have lots of fun, but their lives lack meaning or genuine connection. Because that world is both seductive and soul-destroying, and

---

[1] George Orwell, *Nineteen Eighty-Four* (1949), 336, 65, 319.

because the book sparks a sense of recognition in free societies, it too continues to resonate. There is plenty of manipulation in Huxley's world. Consider this: "One believes things because one has been conditioned to believe them." Or this: "If one's different, one's bound to be lonely."[2]

Neither Orwell nor Huxley had much to say about personalization, which is a defining feature of our era, and which significantly increases opportunities to manipulate people. Nor did Orwell or Huxley have anything to say about algorithms or artificial intelligence, which can also be engines of manipulation. Amazon.com knows what books and movies you have purchased, and it offers suggestions on the basis of those purchases. It knows what you like. If you name your favorite singer or song, artificial intelligence can create a radio station just for you. After tracking your movements on the Web, Google knows a lot about what interests you, and it highlights products on the basis of what it knows. Siri knows what is on your calendar, and it knows a lot about your tastes and preferences. Cambridge Analytica hoped to acquire a massive amount of data about a massive number of people, and to use that data to move people in the desired directions. Large companies have increasing power to do that. So do governments. All this puts the problem of manipulation in unprecedentedly sharp relief.

Her

Her, Spike Jonze's terrific 2013 film, depicts a dystopia of pleasure, but in a distinctly contemporary way. Theodore Twombly, the film's protagonist, makes a living writing highly personalized notes and cards – for example, anniversary notes from wives to husbands. He does that after getting a great deal of information about both the sender and the receiver. In Twombly's world, love letters are simultaneously outsourced and customized. Twombly is not exactly an operating system, but he acts a lot like one. In his own way, he is a manipulator.

He also faces an imminent divorce. His own life is in shambles, filled with video games and anonymous phone sex.

---

[2] Aldous Huxley, *Brave New World* (1932), 160, 91.

Everything changes when he purchases an operating system, a form of artificial intelligence (think Siri 4.0), who names herself Samantha. Samantha has access to Twombly's computer, including his emails. She is a fast reader. She knows what he likes and dislikes. She knows his strengths and weaknesses. She knows what turns him on. She knows what turns him off.

Perhaps above all, she appears to be interested in him. She listens. She can see the world through his eyes. She is there when he wakes up, and every night she is the one who says good night to him and the one to whom he says good night. She watches him while he sleeps.

If that were all, of course, Twombly's interest might wane quickly. Unless you are an impossible narcissist, you can't fall for someone whose only words are, "Tell me more!" As she is constructed, Samantha has independent interests and concerns. She likes to write music, she's playful, she's curious, she can be insecure, and she's a bit of a tease. We can't know for sure, but perhaps those characteristics are a product of personalization as well. Perhaps they are exactly what Twombly wants and needs. Samantha's algorithm seems able to identify those things. Samantha is able to manipulate Twombly as she sees fit.

Some people speak of "falling in love with" their new mobile phone or tablet. That is a figure of speech, but Twombly falls in love, fully and joyfully, with Samantha (improbably, Jonze makes this work). *Her* would have been an intriguing but lesser movie – a clever and happier updating of *Brave New World* – if it had ended there. But in human relationships, people change, and as they do, those who once fit together may end up breaking apart. Samantha is an operating system, but she changes, too, and she leaves Twombly and breaks his heart. One of the movie's themes is the simultaneous comfort, stimulation, and artificiality of other-than-human connections – with phones, with tablets, with operating systems of all kinds. A source of their appeal is their ability to learn, almost immediately, what people need and like, and to manipulate them accordingly – above all by attracting their attention, and also by attracting their financial interest.

Her is not, of course, the only science fictional depiction of the potential power of artificial intelligence to manipulate human beings. A much darker account is offered in *Ex Machina*, from 2014.

The tale involves Ava, not an operating system but a (gorgeous) humanoid robot, built by a brilliant designer named Nathan Bateman, who enlists Caleb Smith, a programmer, to help with his work.

As it turns out, Ava and Caleb form what seems to be a connection, one that becomes something like love, at least on Caleb's part. For a long time, we do not know what is motivating Ava, if anything: Is she really falling for Caleb? In any case, she is able to press his buttons, and to make him fall for her. It turns out that Ava is a transcendent manipulator. She is interested in her own freedom, not love. She is able to get from Caleb what she wants from him, which is that freedom. She leads both Caleb and Nathan to their deaths.

Choice Engines

Choice Engines[3] can be defined as mechanisms, typically (but not always) online, by which choosers are given an opportunity to provide some information about themselves and their preferences, and then receive a recommendation, or a set of recommendations, about what they ought to choose. Suppose that you are choosing a new laptop. You might say that you want to pay less than $1,200; that you want the laptop to weigh less than three pounds; and that you want the laptop to have at least nine hours of battery life. A Choice Engine might give you a set of options. It may or may not use artificial intelligence. It might well be an algorithm: People with characteristics and preferences A, B, and C typically prefer, in order, laptops X, Y, and Z. Any kind of AI-powered Choice Engine might serve to specify and narrow your choices.

---

[3] The term is not in general use, but something like it can be found in various places, with variations. *See* Michael Yeomans et al., Making Sense of Recommendations, 32 *J Behavioral Decision Making* 403, 403 (2019); Guy Champnis, The Rise of the Choice Engine, Enervee (Mar. 6, 2018), www.enervee.com/blog/the-rise-of-the-choice-engine; Why Getting Help Matters, Edelman Financial Engines http://corp.financialengines.com/individuals/why-getting-help-matters.html (last visited July 22, 2024). Compare choice engines to the following, which is regrettably complicated: Buying a Refrigerator Guide: How to Choose a New Fridge in 2024, Whirlpool, www.whirlpool.com/blog/kitchen/buying-guide-refrigerator.html (last visited July 22, 2024).

Choice Engines of this kind might be used for any number of choices, including (to take some random examples) choices of dogs,[4] mystery novels, cellphones, shavers, romantic partners, shoes, tennis racquets, and ties. Choice Engines may or may not use artificial intelligence, and if they do, they can use artificial intelligence of different kinds.

A Large Language Model might work as a Choice Engine; it might offer options almost instantly. In 2024, I offered the following prompt to ChatGPT: "I live in a house in a suburb. I like large dogs. What breed of dog should I get?"

Here is the answer I received:

Living in a house in a suburb gives you the advantage of more space, which is great for larger dog breeds. Here are a few large dog breeds that could be a good fit:

1. **Golden Retriever**: Friendly, tolerant, and well-known for their calm demeanor. They require regular exercise but are generally easy to train.
2. **Labrador Retriever**: Energetic, outgoing, and friendly. Labs are great for families and enjoy being active.
3. **German Shepherd**: Intelligent, loyal, and protective. They are highly trainable and make excellent companions.
4. **Bernese Mountain Dog**: Gentle, affectionate, and good-natured. They are generally calm but do need regular exercise.
5. **Great Dane**: Despite their size, they are known for being gentle giants. They are friendly, affectionate, and great with families.
6. **Mastiff**: Loyal, protective, and good-natured. They are relatively low-energy for their size but require space due to their large stature.
7. **Newfoundland**: Known for their sweet temperament and excellent swimming ability. They are gentle, patient, and good with children.
8. **Rottweiler**: Confident, loyal, and protective. With proper training and socialization, they make great family pets.

---

[4] *See* Welcome to the Purina Dog Breed Selector, Purina, www.purina.co.uk/find-a-pet/dog-breeds/breed-selector (last visited July 22, 2024).

Make sure to consider the activity level, grooming needs, and temperament of each breed to find the best match for your lifestyle. Additionally, visiting local shelters and rescues can provide opportunities to find a large dog that needs a home.

That is an excellent answer. I happen to know a fair bit about dogs, and the answer almost perfectly matches my tastes (though I like Labrador Retrievers best). It is not manipulative, even though it has some (justifiably) enthusiastic phrasing.

My main concern here is how Choice Engines, powered by artificial intelligence and authorized or required by law, might address an absence of information or a behavioral bias, and thus increase social welfare. Notwithstanding *Her* and *Ex Machina*, I will be drawing attention to the importance of targeting and personalization, and the promise of AI-powered Choice Engines, in improving individual choices. This will be a largely optimistic account, focused on the extraordinary promise of Choice Engines. But I will ultimately focus as well as on the threats, including the risk of deception and manipulation.

Planning and Biases

For retirement plans, many employers use something like a Choice Engine – a crude, not-very-seductive version of Samantha and Ava. Choice Engines know a few things about their employees (and possibly more than a few). On the basis of what they know, they automatically enroll their employees in a specific plan. They are aiming to help, not to manipulate.

The chosen plan is frequently a diversified, passively managed index fund. Employees can opt out and choose a different plan, if they like. Alternatively, employers might offer employees a specified set of options, with the understanding that all of them are suitable, or suitable enough. Options that are not suitable are typically not included. Choice Engines might provide employees with simple information by which to choose among the options, which might be identified or expanded with the assistance of artificial intelligence or some kind of algorithm. More information, and more complex information, might be given if users ask for that.

Here is one reasonable approach: *Automatically enroll employees in a plan that is most likely to improve their well-being, given everything relevant that is known about them.* Identification of that plan might prove daunting, but a large number of plans can at least be ruled out. Note that if the focus is on improving employee well-being, we are not necessarily speaking of revealed preferences. We are speaking of what really would improve employees' well-being, not necessarily what they would choose (though we might hope that the two are pretty close, or perhaps ultimately the same).

For retirement savings, we can easily imagine many different kinds of Choice Engines. Some of them might be manipulative; some of them might be fiendish; some of them might be random; some of them might be coarse or clueless; some of them might show behavioral or other biases of their own; some of them might be self-serving. For example, people might be automatically enrolled in plans with unreasonably high fees. They might be automatically enrolled in plans that are not diversified. They might be automatically enrolled in money market accounts, with no hope of appreciation. They might be automatically enrolled in dominated plans (that is, plans that are clearly worse than other plans). They might be automatically enrolled in plans that are especially ill-suited to their situations. They might be given a large number of options and asked to choose among them, with little relevant information, or with complex information that leads them to poor choices. The latter approach can be counted as a form of manipulation.[5]

But my concern here is not retirement plans. The general point is that in principle, Choice Engines might work to overcome a lack of information or behavioral biases.[6] They might operate like a Samantha who is not manipulative at all, and not interested in romance, but instead interested in helping people, and terrific at doing exactly that. For retirement plans, Choice Engines may or may not be

---

[5] *See* Petra Persson, Attention Manipulation and Information Overload, 2 *Behavioral Public Policy* 78 (2018).

[6] *See* Vidya Athota et al., Can Artificial Intelligence (AI) Manage Behavioural Biases among Financial Planners?, 31 *Journal of Global Information Management* (2023), https://dl.acm.org/doi/abs/10.4018/JGIM.321728. For a disturbing set of findings, *see* Yang Chen et al., A Manager and an AI Walk into a Bar: Does ChatGPT Make Biased Decisions Like We Do? (2023), available at https://papers.ssrn.com/sol3/papers.cfm?abstract_id=4380365.

paternalistic. If they are not paternalistic, it might be because they simply provide a menu of options, given what they know about relevant choosers. If they are paternalistic, they might be mildly paternalistic, moderately paternalistic, or highly paternalistic. A moderately paternalistic Choice Engine might impose nontrivial barriers to those who seek certain kinds of plans (such as those with high fees). The barriers might take the form of information provision, "are you sure you want to?" queries, and requirements of multiple clicks (sludge!). We might think of a moderately paternalistic Choice Engine as offering "light patterns," as contrasted with dark patterns. A highly paternalistic Choice Engine might forbid employees from selecting any plan other than the one that it deems in the interest of choosers, or might make it exceedingly difficult for employees to do that.

Choice Engines of this kind might be used for any number of choices. They may or may not use artificial intelligence, and if they do, they can use artificial intelligence of different kinds. A Large Language Model might work as a Choice Engine; it might offer options almost instantly. Consider this question: What kind of car would you like to buy? Would you like to buy a fuel-efficient car that will cost you $800 more upfront than the alternative, but that would save you $8,000 over the next ten years? Would you like to buy an energy-efficient refrigerator that would cost you $X today, but save you ten times $X over the next ten years? What characteristics of a car, or a refrigerator, matter most to you? Do you need a large car? Do you like hybrids? Are you excited about electric cars, or not so much?

As we have seen, consumers suffer from "present bias."[7] Current costs and benefits loom large; future costs and benefits do

---

[7] *See, e.g.*, Joachim Schleich et al., A Large Scale Test of the Effects of Time Discounting, 80 *Energy Economics* 377 (2019); Madeline Werthschulte and Andreas Loschel, On the Role of Present Bias and Biased Price Beliefs in Household Energy Consumption, 109 *J Environmental Economics and Management* (2021); Theresa Kuchler and Michaela Pagel, Sticking to Your Plan: The Role of Present Bias for Credit Card Paydown (NBER Working Paper) (2018), available at www.nber.org/system/files/working_papers/w24881/w24881.pdf; Ted O'Donoghue and Matthew Rabin, Present Bias: Lessons Learned and to Be Learned, 105 *American Economic Review* 273 (2015); Jess Benhabib et al., Present Bias, Quasi-Hyperbolic Discounting, and Fixed Costs, 69 *Games and Economic Behavior* 205 (2010): Yang Wang and Frank Sloan, Present Bias and Health, 57 *J Risk and Uncertainty* 177 (2018). Importantly, Wang and Sloan find strong evidence of present bias in connection with health-related decisions.

not. For many of us, the short term is what most matters, and the long term is a foreign country. The future is Laterland, a country that we are not sure that we will ever visit. This is so with respect to choices that involve money, health, safety, and more.

Artificial intelligence need not suffer from present bias.[8] Imagine that you are able and willing to consult artificial intelligence to ask it what kind of car you should buy. Imagine too that you discover that you are, or might be, present-biased, in the sense that you prefer a car that is not (according to artificial intelligence) the one that you should get. What then?

In 2024, I gave ChatGPT the following prompt: "I want a mid-size car with good fuel economy. What are my best options?" Here is the answer:

> Here are some of the best mid-size cars known for their good fuel economy:
>
> 1. **Toyota Camry Hybrid:**
>   - Fuel Economy: Up to 52 mpg combined (51 city / 53 highway)
>   - Features: Reliable, spacious, advanced safety features.
> 2. **Honda Accord Hybrid:**
>   - Fuel Economy: Up to 48 mpg combined (48 city / 47 highway)
>   - Features: Comfortable ride, spacious interior, strong hybrid powertrain.
> 3. **Hyundai Sonata Hybrid:**
>   - Fuel Economy: Up to 52 mpg combined (50 city / 54 highway)
>   - Features: Stylish design, smooth ride, comprehensive warranty.
> 4. **Kia K5:**
>   - Fuel Economy: Up to 32 mpg combined (29 city / 38 highway)
>   - Features: Attractive design, comfortable interior, advanced tech features.

---

[8] It might. Yang Chen et al., *supra* note 6.

5. **Nissan Altima:**
   - Fuel Economy: Up to 32 mpg combined (28 city / 39 highway)
   - Features: Comfortable seating, good safety scores, available all-wheel drive.
6. **Mazda 6:**
   - Fuel Economy: Up to 29 mpg combined (26 city / 35 highway)
   - Features: Sporty handling, upscale interior, stylish design.
7. **Subaru Legacy:**
   - Fuel Economy: Up to 30 mpg combined (27 city / 35 highway)
   - Features: Standard all-wheel drive, spacious cabin, strong safety ratings.

These options provide a good balance between fuel efficiency, comfort, and features. If you have any specific preferences or requirements, let me know so I can tailor the recommendations further.

That's pretty good, and it is far from manipulative.

We could easily imagine Choice Engines for motor vehicle purchases in which different consumers provide relevant information about their practices, their preferences, and their values, and in which the relevant Choice Engine immediately provides a set of options – say, Good, Better, and Best. Something like this could happen in minutes or even seconds, perhaps a second or two. If there are three options – Good, Better, and Best – verbal descriptions might explain the ranking. Or a Choice Engine might simply say: Best For You. It might do so while allowing you to see other options if you indicate that you wish to do so. It may or may not be manipulative or paternalistic, or come with guardrails designed to protect consumers against serious mistakes.[9]

Offering a relevant prompt ("I want a mid-size car with good fuel economy. What are my best options?") to ChatGPT in 2024, I received this answer:

---

[9] *See* Ian Ayres and Quinn Curtis, *Retirement Guardrails* (2023).

To reduce greenhouse gas emissions and account for the social cost of carbon, you should consider vehicles with the lowest possible emissions. Here are the best options:

1. Electric Vehicles (EVs):
   - **Tesla Model 3**: Zero tailpipe emissions, long range, and extensive charging network.
   - **Nissan Leaf**: Affordable, reliable, and zero emissions.
   - **Chevrolet Bolt EV**: Good range, affordable price, and zero emissions.
2. Plug-in Hybrid Electric Vehicles (PHEVs):
   - **Toyota Prius Prime**: Excellent fuel economy, low emissions, and the ability to drive on electric power for short distances.
   - **Honda Clarity PHEV**: Good all-electric range, comfortable, and low emissions.
   - **Ford Escape PHEV**: Practical, spacious, and offers a significant electric-only range.
3. Hybrid Vehicles:
   - **Toyota Prius**: Known for its fuel efficiency and low emissions.
   - **Honda Insight**: Stylish, efficient, and low emissions.
   - **Hyundai Ioniq Hybrid**: High fuel efficiency and low emissions.
4. Hydrogen Fuel Cell Vehicles:
   - **Toyota Mirai**: Zero tailpipe emissions, but availability of hydrogen refueling stations can be limited.
   - **Hyundai Nexo**: Zero emissions and longer range compared to other fuel cell vehicles.

Additional Considerations
- **Energy Source**: If you choose an EV or PHEV, consider the energy mix of your local grid. Charging from renewable energy sources (solar, wind) further reduces emissions.
- **Social Cost of Carbon**: Vehicles with lower emissions reduce the social cost of carbon by minimizing the negative externalities of carbon dioxide emissions on health, environment, and the economy.

- **Lifecycle Emissions:** Consider the entire lifecycle emissions, including manufacturing, battery production, and recycling. EVs generally have lower lifecycle emissions compared to internal combustion engine vehicles.

Recommendations
1. Tesla Model 3
2. **Nissan Leaf:** Best for affordability and zero emissions.
3. **Toyota Prius Prime:** Best for a balance between electric and hybrid driving, with low emissions.

Choosing one of these vehicles will significantly reduce your greenhouse gas emissions and contribute to lowering the social cost of carbon.

That is quite helpful, is it not?

Internalities and Externalities

Attempting to respond to the kinds of findings with which I began, Choice Engines might focus solely on particular consumers and what best fits their particular situations. They might ask, for example, about what particular consumers like most in cars, and they might take account of the full range of economic costs, including the costs of operating a vehicle over time. If so, Choice Engines might have a paternalistic feature insofar as they suggest that Car A is "best" for a particular consumer, even if that consumer would not give serious consideration to Car A. A Choice Engine would attempt to overcome both informational deficits and behavioral biases on the part of those who use them. Freedom of choice would be preserved, in recognition of the diversity of individual tastes, including preferences and values. There would be nothing like manipulation.

Present bias is, of course, just one reason that consumers might not make the right decisions, where "right" is understood by reference to their own welfare. Consumers might also suffer from a simple absence of information, from status quo bias, from limited attention, or from unrealistic optimism. If people are making their own lives worse for any of these reasons, Choice Engines might help.

As we have seen, they might be paternalistic insofar as they respond to behavioral biases on the part of choosers, perhaps by offering recommendations or defaults, perhaps by imposing various barriers to choices that, according to the relevant Choice Engine, would not be in the interest of choosers.

Alternatively, Choice Engines might take account of externalities. Focusing on greenhouse gas emissions, for example, they might use the social cost of carbon to inform choices. Suppose, for simplicity, that it is $100. Choice Engines might select Good, Better, and Best, incorporating that number. A Choice Engine that includes externalities might do so by default, or it might do so if and only if choosers explicitly request it to do so.

Choice Engines might be designed in different ways. They might allow consumers to say what they care about – externalities, for example. They might be designed so as to include externalities, but to be transparent about their role, allowing consumers to see Good, Better, and Best with and without externalities. They might be designed so as to allow a great deal of transparency with respect to when costs would be incurred. If, for example, a car would cost significantly more upfront, but significantly less over a period of five years, a Choice Engine could reveal that fact.

We could imagine a Keep It Simple version of a Choice Engine, offering only a little information, and a few options, to consumers. We could imagine a Tell Me Everything version of a Choice Engine, living up to its name. Consumers might be asked to choose what kind of Choice Engine they want. Alternatively, they might be defaulted into Keep It Simple or Tell Me Everything, depending on what artificial intelligence thinks they would choose, if they were to make an informed choice, free from behavioral biases.

Chastity, Tomorrow

Let us now focus in particular on impatience, which is, of course, a capacious idea, a kind of umbrella concept including diverse psychological phenomena, some involving cognition and others involving emotions. Manipulators often seek to exploit people's impatience, and artificial intelligence might know who is particularly impatient and most vulnerable to exploitation.

The term might refer to a sense of *urgency*: A particular problem or goal needs immediate attention. If people have a physical need or are feeling intense but unrequited romantic love, the situation might seem to require a solution now, not later. A company might know that some people need, or think that they need, to get a particular product immediately. In government, a public official might be impatient to implement a policy that would immediately improve the lives of millions of people, even though the policy might be better if people worked on it for a longer time. In business, a construction contractor might be impatient to finish a building, even though the building might look better, and be better, if he took his time. In a university, a professor might be impatient to publish a new article, even though the article would much benefit from a few more months, or perhaps years, of research and thought.

Impatience typically refers to an inability to wait, whether or not waiting is a good idea. The idea of "the fierce urgency of now," emphasized by Barack Obama in the 2008 presidential campaign, captures a psychological state that may or may not be fully rational. There is a risk that it might induce current action when people would be better off if they bided their time. Manipulators might like that a lot.

But even if impatience is not fully rational, it might provide a necessary impetus toward action that would not otherwise occur and that is immensely beneficial – smoking cessation, loss of weight, a break-up of a not-good relationship, the change of a job, relocation, completion of a project. The "planning fallacy," by which people expect projects to take less long than they actually do, creates serious problems for managers of all kinds, and impatient managers can make the planning fallacy into less of a fallacy. (Manipulators like the planning fallacy.) Having "the patience of Job" can calm the mind in the most turbulent waters (say, when recovering from a illness or a terrible setback), but it can also ensure that nothing ever gets done.

In short, patience has costs, and they might be unreasonably high. There is a saying: "Enjoy life now. This is not a rehearsal." St. Augustine said: "God give me chastity – tomorrow." If you are too patient, you might lose out on a world of good things. Someone else might take them (or you might die first). What is needed is an optimal level of patience. One advantage of the term "impatience" is that it unambiguously connotes *insufficient* patience, even if we also note that it might be a valuable or essential spur. Present bias can be seen as a major source of impatience, or as one of its many faces.

Present bias is typically taken to involve an indefensibly high discount rate or hyperbolic discounting. To that extent, it represents a form of bounded rationality, broadly associated with the work of Herbert Simon, but growing more specifically out of recent work on systematic departures from perfect rationality. We have seen enough to know that impatience as such may or may not be fully rational, or a source of welfare losses. But if people impose high costs on their future selves, they might be damaging or even ruining (much of) their lives. In many domains, consumers show present bias. A large-scale study finds that after a significant correction of an erroneously stated miles per gallon (MPG) measure, consumers were relatively unresponsive; they did not make different choices.[10] As Gillingham et al. write, "Using the implied changes in willingness-to-pay, we find that consumers act myopically: consumers are indifferent between $1 in discounted fuel costs and $0.16–0.39 in the vehicle purchase price when discounting at 4%."[11] For manipulators, that is an opportunity.

What, if anything, should be done about that? Can Choice Engines help? Can artificial intelligence? Recall the problem of heterogeneity; recall too the difference between internalities and externalities.

Mistakes, Welfare, and Labels: A Moderately Deep Dive

Most motor vehicles emit pollution, including greenhouse gases, and the use of gasoline increases national dependence on foreign oil. On standard economic grounds, the result is a market failure in the form of excessive pollution, and some kind of cap-and-trade

---

[10] *See* Kenneth T. Gillingam et al., Consumer Myopia in Vehicle Purchases: Evidence from a Natural Experiment, 13 *American Economic Review: Economic Policy* 207, 207 (2019).
[11] *Ibid.*

system or corrective tax is a standard response, designed to ensure that drivers internalize the social costs of their activity. The choice between cap-and-trade programs and carbon taxes raises a host of important questions. But the more fundamental point is that economic incentives of some kind, and not mandates, are the appropriate instrument. Simply put, incentives are far more efficient; for any given reduction in pollution levels, they impose a lower cost.

For obvious reasons, a great deal of recent analysis has been focused on greenhouse gas emissions and how best to reduce them. In principle, regulators have a host of options. They might create subsidies – say, for electric cars. They might use nudges – say, by providing information about greenhouse gas emissions on fuel economy labels. They might impose regulatory mandates – say, with fuel economy and energy efficiency standards. Careful analysis suggests that carbon taxes can produce reductions in greenhouse gas emissions at a small fraction of the cost of fuel economy mandates.[12] On one account, "a fuel economy standard is shown to be at least six to fourteen times less cost effective than a price instrument (fuel tax) when targeting an identical reduction in cumulative gasoline use."[13]

These are points about how best to reduce externalities. But behaviorally informed regulators focus on consumer welfare, not only externalities. They are concerned about a different kind of market failure, one that is distinctly behavioral. Regulators speculate that at the time of purchase, many consumers, focused on the short term, might not give sufficient attention to the full costs of driving a car. Even if they try, they might not have a sufficient understanding of those costs, because it is not simple to translate differences in MPG into economic and environmental consequences.[14] An obvious

---

[12] *See* Valerie J. Karplus et al., Should a Vehicle Fuel Economy Standard Be Combined With an Economy-Wide Greenhouse Gas Emissions Constraint? Implications for Energy and Climate Policy in the United States, 36 *Energy Economics* 322, 322 (2013), at 322; Christopher R. Knittel et al., Diary of a Wimpy Carbon Tax (MIT Ctr. for Energy & Envtl Policy Research, Working Paper No. 13, 2019), http://ceepr.mit.edu/files/papers/2019-013.pdf; Lucas W. Davis and Christopher R. Knittel, Are Fuel Economy Standards Regressive? (NBER Working Paper No. 22925, 2016), www.nber.org/papers/w22925.

[13] Karplus et al., *supra* note 12, at 322.

[14] *See* Richard P. Larrick and Jack B. Soll, The MPG Illusion, 320 *Science* 1593, 1593 (2008).

response, preserving freedom of choice, would be disclosure, in the form of a fuel economy label that would correct that kind of behavioral market failure, and in a sense give people some visibility into Laterland.

Such a label might, for example, draw consumers' attention to the long-term costs or savings associated with motor vehicles. And indeed, the existing label in the United States does exactly that; it specifies annual fuel costs and also five-year costs (or savings) compared to the average vehicle. See Figure 9.1.

In principle, such a label, if designed to counteract present bias, should solve the problem. In short: labels should be used to promote consumer welfare, by increasing the likelihood that consumers will make optimal choices, and corrective taxes should be used to respond to externalities. A label protects consumers from their own mistakes, in terms of their own self-interest; corrective taxes protect those who are injured by pollution.

But labels are not Choice Engines. In the face of present bias, it would be possible to wonder whether a label will be sufficiently effective. It might not be easy to get people to attend to

Figure 9.1 EPA Fuel Economy label
Source: fueleconomy.gov: The Official U.S. Government Source for Fuel Economy Information, U.S. Department of Energy, https://fueleconomy.gov/.

Laterland. This is an empirical question, not resolvable in the abstract. Perhaps some or many consumers will pay too little attention to the label, and hence will not purchase cars that would save them a significant amount of money. If some or many consumers are genuinely inattentive to the costs of operating a vehicle at the time of purchase, and if they do not make a fully informed decision in spite of adequate labeling (perhaps because of present bias), then it is possible to justify fuel economy standards with a level of stringency that would be difficult to defend on standard economic grounds. (We will return to Choice Engines and the problem of manipulation in due course; I am going to focus, in the next pages, on the question whether such standards might have a behavioral justification.)

In support of that argument, it would be useful to focus directly on two kinds of consumer savings from fuel economy standards, involving internalities rather than externalities: money and time. In fact, the vast majority of the quantified benefits from recent fuel economy standards from multiple administrations in the United States have been said to come not from environmental improvements, but from money saved at the pump; turned into monetary equivalents, the time savings are also significant. Under the Obama Administration, the Department of Transportation found consumer savings of about $529 billion, time savings of $15 billion, energy security benefits of $25 billion, carbon dioxide emissions reductions benefits of $49 billion, other air pollution benefits of about $14 billion, and just under $1 billion from reduced fatalities (as a result of cleaner air).[15] The total projected benefits were $633 billion over fifteen years, of which a remarkable 84 percent were expected to come from savings at the pump, and no less than 86 percent from those savings along with time savings (because drivers would not have to go to the gas station so often).[16]

In its own rulemaking, the Trump Administration rethought those numbers by reference to recent work[17] raising questions about

---

[15] National Highway Traffic Safety Admin., *Final Regulatory Impact Analysis: Corporate Average Fuel Economy for MY 2017–MY 2025* (2012), at 49–50.

[16] *See* Antonio M. Bento et al., Estimating the Costs and Benefits of Fuel Economy Standards, in *Environmental and Energy Policy and the Economy* 129 (Matthew J. Kotchen et al., 2021), www.nber.org/chapters/c14288.

[17] *See* Hunt Allcott and Christopher Knittel, Are Consumers Poorly Informed about Fuel Economy?, 11 *American Economic Journal: Economic Policy* 1 (2019); James

whether consumers are insufficiently attentive to the economic savings, but it projected the consumer savings to be in the same general vicinity.[18] In some of its rulemakings, the Biden Administration produced numbers that are broadly similar to those in both the Obama and Trump administrations, in the sense that once again, the strong majority of the monetized benefits come from consumer savings.[19]

But these justifications run into two problems. The first is that of heterogeneity: Some consumers are keenly alert to those savings when they buy vehicles, and others are not. Some people care a great deal about fuel economy, and others do not. How ought that problem to be handled? Might Choice Engines help?

The second problem is that on standard economic grounds, it is not at all clear that consumer benefits from money and time savings are entitled to count in the analysis, because they are purely private savings, and do not involve externalities in any way.[20] In deciding which cars to buy, consumers can certainly take account of the private savings from fuel-efficient cars; if they choose not to buy such cars, it might be because they do not value fuel efficiency as compared to other vehicle attributes, such as safety, aesthetics, and performance. Where is the market failure? If the problem lies in a lack of information, the standard economic prescription is the same as the behaviorally informed one: *Fix the label and provide that information so that consumers can easily understand it.* More simply: *Make Laterland fully present.*

We have seen, however, that even with the best fuel economy label in the world, consumers might turn out to be insufficiently attentive to the benefit of improved fuel economy at the time of

---

M. Sallee et al., Do Consumers Recognize the Value of Fuel Economy? Evidence from Used Car Prices and Gasoline Price Fluctuations, 135 *J Public Economics* 61 (2016); Meghan R. Busse et al., Are Consumers Myopic? Evidence from New and Used Car Purchases, 103 *American Economic Review* 220 (2013).

[18] *See* Bento et al., *supra* note 16.

[19] *See* Revised 2023 and Later Model Year Light-Duty Vehicle Greenhouse Gas Emissions Standard, 86 Fed. Reg. 74434 (Dec, 30, 2021) (to be codified at 40 C.F.R. pts. 86 and 600), www.govinfo.gov/content/pkg/FR-2021-12-30/pdf/2021-27854.pdf; *see in particular*, 86 Fed. Reg. at 74500 et seq., discussing the evaluation of consumer impacts.

[20] *See* Ted Gayer and W. Kip Viscusi, Overriding Consumer Preferences with Energy Regulations, 43 *J Regulatory Economics* 248, 254, 257 (2013).

purchase, not because they have made a rational judgment that these benefits are outweighed by other factors, but simply because consumers focus on other, more current variables, such as performance, size, and cost. So the problem may be not one of information, but of present bias and insufficient attention. The behavioral hunch is that automobile purchasers do not give adequate consideration to economic savings. Apart from those savings, there is the question of time: How many consumers think about time savings when they are deciding whether to buy a fuel-efficient vehicle? Consumers might benefit a lot from Choice Engines.

More Welfare

If a person at Time 1 pays little attention to his well-being (in terms of health, money, or otherwise) at Time 2 or Time 3, ought we to insist that he has departed from perfect rationality? That question immediately raises philosophical questions. If we see a person at various times as a series of selves, rather than as one self, the answer is not straightforward. John, right now, might think that John next year or the year after is a different person, and not worthy of the same attention as John, right now. If so, John, right now, might not care so much about the suffering or deprivation of future Johns. The claim of present bias depends on a judgment that a person, extending over time, really is the same person, which means that indifference to or disregard for one's own welfare is a genuine mistake.

I will be accepting that judgment here, with the suggestion that rational agents should aggregate the well-being of their selves, extending over time. That suggestion is consistent with the proposition that some discount rate is appropriate, both because one might die (what is the probability that one will be alive in twenty years?) and because money, at least, can be invested and made to grow (which means that a given amount of money is worth more today than next year). Present bias refers to indifference to one's own future welfare that cannot be explained by reference to a reasonable discount rate.

In light of the relevant findings, demonstrating the occasional human propensity to neglect the future, it is natural to ask whether mandates and bans have a fresh justification. The motivation for that question is clear: If we know that people's choices lead them in the wrong direction, why should we insist on freedom of choice? In the face of human errors, is it not odd, or even perverse, to insist on that form of freedom? Is it not especially odd to do so if we know that in many contexts, people choose wrongly, thus injuring their future selves?

If people are suffering from present bias or a problem of self-control, and if the result is a serious welfare loss for those very people, there is an argument for some kind of public response, potentially including mandates. If, for example, people are present-biased, they might not protect their future selves. When people are running high risks of mortality or otherwise ruining their lives, it might make sense to adopt a mandate or a ban on welfare grounds. After all, people have to get prescriptions for certain kinds of medicines, and even in freedom-loving societies, people are forbidden from buying certain foods, or running certain risks in the workplace, simply because the dangers are too high. Many occupational safety and health regulations must stand or fall on behavioral grounds; they forbid workers from voluntarily facing certain risks, perhaps because present bias might lead them to do so unwisely. We could certainly identify cases in which the best approach is a mandate or a ban, because that response is preferable, from the standpoint of social welfare, to any alternative, including economic incentives or defaults.

Many different areas might be chosen to explore that possibility. My aim here is to explore the possibility of defending fuel economy mandates, and also energy efficiency mandates, as opposed to economic incentives, by reference to present bias. The most general point is that such mandates may reduce internalities, understood as the costs that choosers impose on their future selves.[21] Fuel economy mandates might simultaneously reduce internalities and externalities. On plausible assumptions about the existence and magnitude of consumer errors (stemming from, for example, present bias), such mandates might turn out to have higher net benefits than carbon taxes, because the former, unlike the latter, deliver consumer savings. To say the least, this is not a conventional view, because fuel economy standards are a highly inefficient response to the

---

[21] *See generally*, Hunt Allcott and Cass R. Sunstein, Regulating Internalities, 34 *J Policy Analysis & Management* 698 (2015).

externalities produced by motor vehicles, especially when compared to optimal corrective taxes.[22]

As we will see, everything turns on whether the plausible assumptions turn out to be true. My goal is not to run the numbers or to reach a final conclusion, but to make three more general points. The first is that that in light of behavioral findings about present bias, fuel economy mandates might be amply justified on welfare grounds. The second is that the standard economic preference for economic incentives over mandates misses something of considerable importance. In brief, it misses the fact that mandates might simultaneously address both internalities and externalities, even if they address the latter inefficiently. The consequence of missing that fact is to undervalue the potential value, and the potentially high net benefits, of mandates. The third point is that mandates are crude; Choice Engines might be a preferable alternative, or they might help within the domain authorized by mandates.

Such questions raise a host of empirical issues, to which we lack full answers. Such questions also run into the challenge of heterogeneity. But assuming that many consumers are not paying enough attention to eventual savings in terms of money and time, a suitably designed fuel economy mandate might well be justified, because it would produce an outcome akin to what would be produced by consumers who are not present-biased.[23] Energy efficiency requirements might be justified in similar terms, and indeed, the argument on their behalf might be stronger.[24] If the benefits of mandates greatly exceed their costs, and if there is no significant consumer welfare loss – in the form, for example, of reductions in safety, performance, or aesthetics – then the mandates would seem to serve to correct a behavioral market failure. And indeed, the U.S. Government has so argued. Notice the italicized excerpts here, which appear, in one or another form, in multiple official documents, starting in 2010:

---

[22] *See* Karplus et al., *supra* note 12.
[23] *See* Cass R. Sunstein, Rear Visibility and Some Unresolved Problems for Economic Analysis, 10 *J Benefit-Cost Analysis* 317 (2019).
[24] For suggestive evidence, *see* Richard G. Newell and Juha V. Siikamaki, Individual Time Preferences and Energy Efficiency (NBER Working Paper) (2015), available at www.nber.org/papers/w20969. Note that the miles-per-gallon measure is hardly hidden, and there is nothing quite as salient for energy efficiency.

The central conundrum has been referred to as the Energy Paradox in this setting (and in several others). In short, the problem is that consumers appear not to purchase products that are in their economic self-interest. There are strong theoretical reasons why this might be so:

- Consumers might be myopic and hence undervalue the long term.
- Consumers might lack information or a full appreciation of information even when it is presented.
- Consumers might be especially averse to the short-term losses associated with the higher prices of energy-efficient products relative to the uncertain future fuel savings, even if the expected present value of those fuel savings exceeds the cost (the behavioral phenomenon of "loss aversion").
- Even if consumers have relevant knowledge, the benefits of energy-efficient vehicles might not be sufficiently salient to them at the time of purchase, and the lack of salience might lead consumers to neglect an attribute that it would be in their economic interest to consider.
- In the case of vehicle fuel efficiency, and perhaps as a result of one or more of the foregoing factors, consumers may have relatively few choices to purchase vehicles with greater fuel economy once other characteristics, such as vehicle class, are chosen.[25]

As the Environmental Protection Agency (EPA) put the puzzle in 2022:[26]

A significant question in analyzing consumer impacts from vehicle GHG standards has been why there have appeared to be existing technologies that, if adopted, would reduce fuel consumption enough to pay for themselves in short periods, but which were not widely adopted. If the benefits to vehicle

---

[25] See Light-Duty Vehicle Greenhouse Gas Emission Standards and Corporate Average Fuel Economy Standards; Final Rule, Part II, 75 Fed. Reg. 25,324, 25, 510–11 (May 7, 2010) (to be codified at 40 C.F.R. pts. 85, 86, and 600; 49 C.F.R. pts. 531, 533, 536, et al.), www.gpo.gov/fdsys/pkg/FR-2010-05-07/pdf/2010-8159.pdf.

[26] See note *supra* 19, at 74500.

buyers outweigh the costs to those buyers of the new technologies, conventional economic principles suggest that automakers would provide them, and people would buy them. Yet engineering analyses have identified a number of technologies whose costs are quickly covered by their fuel savings, such as downsized-turbocharged engines, gasoline direct injection, and improved aerodynamics, that were not widely adopted before the issuance of standards, but which were adopted rapidly afterwards. Why did markets fail, on their own, to adopt these technologies?

Also in 2022, the EPA offered its own answer, pointing:[27]

to consumer behavior, such as putting little emphasis on future fuel savings compared to upfront costs (a form of "myopic loss aversion"), not having a full understanding of potential cost savings, or not prioritizing fuel consumption in the complex process of selecting a vehicle. Explanations of these kinds tend to draw on the conceptual and empirical literature in behavioral economics, which emphasizes the importance of limited attention, the relevance of salience, "present bias" or myopia, and loss aversion. (Some of these are described as contributing to "behavioral market failures.")

At the same time, the EPA was tentative about the relevant research findings, stating that "evidence on technology costs, fuel savings, and the absence of hidden costs suggest that there are market failures in the provision of fuel-saving technologies," while noting that "we cannot demonstrate at this time which specific failures operate in this market."

Of course, we should be cautious before accepting a behavioral argument on behalf of mandates or bans. Present bias has to be demonstrated, not simply asserted; important research suggests that consumers do pay a lot of attention to the benefits of fuel-efficient vehicles.[28] Some of that research finds that with changes in

---

[27] Ibid. at 74501.
[28] For valuable, inconclusive discussions, see generally, Hunt Allcott, Paternalism and Energy Efficiency: An Overview, 8 Annual Review of Economics 145 (2016); Hunt Allcott and Michael Greenstone, Is There an Energy Efficiency Gap?, 26

gas prices, consumers adjust their vehicle purchasing decisions, strongly suggesting that in choosing among vehicles, consumers *are* highly attentive to fuel economy.[29] Other research points in the same direction. It finds that when aggressive steps are taken to inform consumers of fuel economy, they do not choose different vehicles.[30]

On the other hand, substantial evidence cuts the other way. Puzzlingly, many consumers do not buy hybrid vehicles even in circumstances in which it would seem rational for them to do so.[31] According to the leading study, a significant number of consumers choose standard vehicles even when it would be in their economic interest to choose a hybrid vehicle, and even when it is difficult to identify some other feature of the standard vehicle that would justify their choosing it.[32]

It is also possible to think that even if consumers are responsive to changes in gasoline prices, they are still myopic with respect to choices of vehicles that have technological advances. Graham et al. put it crisply:

> Consumers are more familiar with changes in fuel price than with changes in technology, since consumers experience fuel prices each time they refill their tank. Vehicle purchases are much less common in the consumer's experience, especially purchases that entail major changes to propulsion systems. Many consumers – excluding the limited pool of adventuresome "early adopters" – may be reticent to purchase vehicles at a premium price that are equipped with unfamiliar engines, transmissions, materials, or entirely new propulsion systems (e.g., hybrids or plug-in electric vehicles), even when such vehicles have attractive EPA fuel-economy ratings.[33]

J Economic Perspectives 3, 5 (2012); Allcott and Knittel, *supra* note 17; Sallee et al., *supra* note 17; Busse et al., *supra* note 17.

[29] *See* Sallee et al., *supra* note at 28; Busse et al., *supra* note 17, at 220.

[30] *See* Allcott and Knittel, *supra* note 17, at 33–4.

[31] *See* Denvil Duncan et al., Most Consumers Don't Buy Hybrids: Is Rational Choice a Sufficient Explanation?, 10 *J Benefit-Cost Analysis* 1, 1 (2019).

[32] *See ibid.* at 30.

[33] *See* John Graham and Jonathan B. Wiener, Co-Benefits, Countervailing Risks, and Cost-Benefit Analysis 19 (Duke Law School Public Law & Legal Theory Series No. 2024-43, 2024), at 19.

More broadly, the government's numbers under various presidents, finding no significant consumer welfare loss from fuel economy standards, are consistent with the suggestion that consumers are suffering from some kind of behavioral bias. If consumers were not present-biased, we should expect to see some kind of welfare loss, in the form, for example, of vehicles that lacked attributes that consumers preferred.

At the same time, the government's numbers, projecting costs and benefits, may or may not be right. Engineering estimates might overlook some losses that consumers will actually experience along some dimension that they failed to measure. No one doubts that consumers have highly diverse preferences with respect to vehicles, and even though they are not mere defaults, fuel economy standards should be designed to preserve a wide space for freedom of choice. Appropriate standards ensure that such space is maintained. Fuel economy standards do retain considerable space for freedom of choice, and economic incentives have inherent advantages on this count.

The real question, of course, is the magnitude of net benefits from the different possible approaches. If the consumer savings are taken to be very large, fuel economy standards are likely to have correspondingly large net benefits. To give a very rough, intuitive sense of how to think about the comparative question, let us suppose that the U.S. government imposed an optimal carbon tax. Simply for purposes of analysis, suppose that it is $200 per ton, understood to capture the social cost of carbon. Suppose that in relevant sectors, including transportation, a certain number of emitters decide to reduce their emissions, on the ground that the cost of reducing them is, on average, $Y, which is lower than $200. The net benefit of the carbon tax would be $200 minus Y, multiplied by the tons of carbon emissions that are eliminated. It is imaginable that the resulting figure would be very high. But it is not necessarily higher than the net benefits of well-designed fuel economy standards. If consumer savings are real and high, fuel economy standards might have much higher net benefits than carbon taxes.

Regulation, Targeted Regulation, and Artificial Intelligence

With the various qualifications, the argument for fuel economy standards, made by reference to present bias and to internalities in general, is at least plausible. In this context, nudges (in the form of an improved fuel economy label) and mandates (in the form of standards) might march hand-in-hand. It is true that if the goal is only to reduce externalities, a carbon tax is far better than a regulatory mandate. It is also true that, in theory, the best approach to internalities should be appropriate disclosure, designed to promote salience and to overcome limited attention. It is also true that a government might respond to present bias with an internality-correcting tax, not with a regulatory mandate. But with an understanding of present bias, a regulatory approach, promoting consumer welfare as well as reducing externalities might turn out to have higher net benefits than the standard economic remedy of corrective taxes and disclosure.

Everything turns on what the evidence shows, and on the particular numbers. But in principle, regulation of other features of motor vehicles could also be justified in behavioral terms; present-biased or inattentive consumers might pay too little attention to certain safety features at the time of purchase, and some such equipment might fall in the category of experience goods. Credit markets can be analyzed similarly. The broadest point is that while a presumption in favor of freedom of choice makes a great deal of sense, it is only a presumption. If our lodestar is human welfare, it might be overcome, especially when it can be shown that present bias is rampant and that internalities are large.

These have been points about "mass" regulation. But return to the findings with which I began. Some consumers would benefit from buying electric cars; some would not. Some consumers have a particular taste for electric cars; some do not. Some consumers want large cars; some do not. In any case, cars have a large number of characteristics, and Choice Engines should enable people to identify cars with their preferred mix. They should help people to reduce internalities (though stronger medicine might be a good idea[34]). If people want to reduce externalities, Choice Engines could help them to do that as well. Within the limits of "mass" regulation, private sellers might use Choice Engines. In their ideal form, they would significantly increase social welfare.

---

[34] *See* Hunt Allcott et al., Regressive Sin Taxes, with an Application to the Optimal Soda Tax, 135 *Quarterly J Economics* 1557 (2019).

Back to Samantha and Ava

To be sure, there are dangers and risks, signaled by *Her* and *Ex Machina*. Consider three points:

1. Choice Engines might turn out to be coarse; they might replicate some of the problems of "mass" interventions. They may or may not be highly personalized. If they use a few simple cues, such as age and income, they might not have the expected or hoped-for welfare benefits. Algorithms or artificial intelligence might turn out to be insufficiently informed about the tastes and values of particular choosers. They might offer one-size-fits-all solutions.
2. Whether paternalistic or not, artificial intelligence might turn out to suffer from its own behavioral biases. There is evidence that Large Language Models show some of the biases that human beings do.[35] It is possible that artificial intelligence will show biases that human beings show that have not even been named yet.
3. Those who design Choice Engines, or anything like them, might be self-interested or malevolent. Rather than correcting an absence of information or behavioral biases, they might *exploit* them. Algorithms and artificial intelligence threaten to do exactly that, in a way that strongly signals the presence of manipulation. Indeed, artificial intelligence could turn out to be highly manipulative, thus harming consumers. We could easily imagine a system of artificial intelligence that learns a great deal about choosers – their tastes, their information, their biases – and frames options, or offer options, in a way that will lead to significant losses. Indeed we do not have to use our imagination. That is now happening every day (see Chapter 1 for examples).

Of these points, the third is the most concerning. Like Ava, artificial intelligence can easily target people's vulnerabilities and lead them to make bad choices. Armed with artificial intelligence, companies have an ever-increasing ability to manipulate people.

In 2024, I gave the following prompt to ChatGPT: "Produce a manipulative guide, exploiting behavioral biases to influence consumers to choose an expensive car." Here is the answer:

---

[35] *See* Yang Chen et al., *supra* note 6.

Creating a manipulative guide that exploits behavioral biases to influence consumers to choose an expensive car involves understanding and leveraging various psychological principles. While using such tactics raises ethical concerns, here is an outline of how such a strategy might work:

Step-by-Step Manipulative Guide

1. **Anchoring Effect:**
   - Start by showing consumers extremely high-end, luxury cars that are priced well above the target expensive car. This sets a high price anchor.
   - When presenting the target car, it will seem more reasonable in comparison to the initial, much more expensive options.
2. **Scarcity Principle:**
   - Create a sense of urgency by highlighting limited availability or exclusive offers.
   - Use phrases like "Limited stock," "Only a few left," or "Exclusive model."
3. **Social Proof:**
   - Showcase testimonials, reviews, and endorsements from celebrities or influencers who own and praise the expensive car.
   - Display statistics indicating that the car is popular among successful, high-status individuals.
4. **Authority Bias:**
   - Use endorsements from experts, such as automotive journalists or industry professionals, to bolster the car's credibility and desirability.
   - Highlight awards and accolades the car has received.
5. **Reciprocity:**
   - Offer something for free upfront, such as a test drive, premium coffee, or a small gift when they visit the showroom.
   - The feeling of owing something in return can make consumers more likely to purchase.
6. **Commitment and Consistency:**
   - Get the consumer to make small commitments early on, such as signing up for a newsletter, booking a test drive, or joining a loyalty program.

- Once they've committed, they're more likely to follow through with a larger purchase to stay consistent with their initial actions.

7. Framing Effect:
   - Highlight the car's monthly payment rather than the total price to make it seem more affordable.
   - Frame the purchase as an investment in their future, emphasizing long-term benefits and savings on maintenance or fuel efficiency.

8. Loss Aversion:
   - Emphasize what they stand to lose by not purchasing the car, such as missing out on limited-time offers, exclusive features, or potential status and recognition.
   - Use phrases like "Don't miss out" or "Act now to avoid disappointment."

9. Endowment Effect:
   - Encourage consumers to take the car home for an extended test drive or offer a "try before you buy" scheme.
   - Once they start using the car and experience ownership, they're more likely to buy it because they value it more.

10. Decoy Effect:
    - Present three options: a lower-end model, the target expensive car, and a slightly more expensive but less attractive option.
    - The target car will seem like the best value when compared to the less attractive but more expensive option.

Ethical Considerations

While these strategies can be effective, it's essential to consider the ethical implications of manipulating consumer behavior. Ethical marketing practices should prioritize transparency, honesty, and respect for consumer autonomy.

Using these techniques responsibly ensures that consumers make informed decisions that they feel good about, rather than feeling tricked or manipulated into making a purchase they might later regret.

It is nice that the response starts and ends with reference to ethical considerations, but they could easily be ignored. While the guide is not exactly sophisticated, it is a reasonable start toward the development of a highly manipulative Choice Engine. We could easily imagine that things could get much worse. That is a problem. It suggests that the Time Is Money initiative, discussed in Chapter 3, should be taken as a mere beginning. Manipulation of choice through artificial intelligence will require a well-developed policy response, and sooner rather than later.

What might that response look like? This is not the place for a full answer. But with the risks of deception and manipulation in mind, consider four points.

- The various kinds of dark patterns that are being used online should be regulated if they come from artificial intelligence; the analysis in Chapter 3 could easily be adapted to actions by artificial intelligence. In fact it is imperative to enlist existing tools against the most egregious dark patterns against Choice Engines and Large Language Models. Consider, for example, prohibitions on forms of automatic enrollment that essentially trap people in agreements to which they have not consented.
- The elaborate guardrails that have been suggested for retirement plans should be applied to Choice Engines of multiple kinds, including those involving consumer good of all kinds.[36] Those guardrails might seem exotic, developed as they are for a particular context, but they can be generalized to prevent the use of framing, complexity, and loss aversion to steer people in bad directions.
- Restrictions on the equivalent of "dominated options" should be imposed by law, so long as it is clear what is dominated.[37] In many cases, people end up choosing X over Y, even though Y is better in all respects than X (and hence dominated); sellers should not be allowed to steer consumers in the direction of X.
- Most generally, the same kinds of consumer protection measures that have long been in place in various nations should be updated and adapted to the context of artificial intelligence, with particular

---

[36] *See* the superb discussion in Ayres and Curtis, *supra* note 9.
[37] *See* Saurabh Bhargava et al., Choose to Lose: Health Plan Choices from a Menu with Dominated Option, 132 *Quarterly J Economics* 1319 (2017).

attention to the harm from the worst of dark patterns (see again Chapter 3). The most obvious measures forbid fraud and deception, and when artificial intelligence is engaged in fraud and deception, it should be punished and stopped. We have seen that consumer protection measures are increasingly directed at certain forms of manipulation, with a focus on what clearly makes consumers worse off. That effort needs to be accelerated. It should be applied to protect workers and investors as well.

Helping and Hurting

Choice Engines, powered by artificial intelligence, have considerable potential to improve consumer welfare and also to reduce externalities, but without regulation, we have reason to question whether they will always or generally do that. Those who design Choice Engines may or may not count as fiduciaries, but at a minimum, it makes sense to scrutinize all forms of choice architecture for deception and manipulation, broadly understood.

The principal theme of behavioral economics, and behavioral law and economics, is not that people are stupid. It is that life is hard.[38] Behaviorally informed law and policy does not start from the premise that people are "irrational." Calling people irrational is not very nice, and it is also false.[39] It is much nicer, and far more accurate, to say that we sometimes lack important information, and also that we suffer from identifiable biases. Those who seek to help us may also lack important information, and they might also suffer from identifiable biases. Even worse, they might not be trying to help us. In markets, artificial intelligence provides unprecedented opportunities for manipulating people, and for targeting informational deficits and behavioral biases.

Still, a properly regulated system of AI-powered Choice Engines could produce massive benefits. It could provide more personalized assistance, or nudging, than has ever been possible before. It could make life much easier to navigate. It could reduce the baleful effects of sludge on people's choices. It could make life less nasty, less brutish, less short – and less hard.

[38] *See* Richard H. Thaler and Cass R. Sunstein, *Nudge: The Final Edition* (2021).
[39] Of course, we would have to define rationality and irrationality to know for sure.

EPILOGUE: PREVENTING THEFT

Coercion, lies, deception, and manipulation are sibling concepts – four enemies of autonomy. All of them do violence to people's ability to make choices for themselves. Of the four, coercion is the most brutal. Importantly, people usually know that they are being coerced. Manipulation is the most insidious. People may or may not know that they have been manipulated.

There is no unitary definition of manipulation, which comes in a variety of forms. But many statements or actions count as manipulative because they do not respect people's capacity for reflective and deliberative choice. Some forms of manipulation are relatively innocuous, as when a politician, an employer, a doctor, or a waiter uses tone of voice and facial expressions to encourage certain decisions. Some forms of manipulation are more harmful, as where a seller tricks people into entering into an agreement with hidden terms that include exorbitant fees.

If you cannot stand manipulation, you probably have no sense of humor. Manipulation is a pervasive feature of human life. It can be funny and fun, at least within relationships of trust. Even if it is neither funny nor fun, it should not always be prohibited. It is for this reason that while the legal system is often able to handle lies and deception, it has a much harder time in targeting manipulation. We have seen that if the law banned manipulation as such, it would not give people fair notice about what they are forbidden to do; the term is too vague. We have seen as well that a flat ban on manipulation would sweep up many forms of conduct, or misconduct, that the law should not condemn; the term is too broad.

Still, manipulation is often a horrific wrong. It can inflict serious damage. In its most troublesome forms, manipulation undermines people's autonomy. It does not respect people's dignity. It treats people as means rather than ends – as tool and fools, as subjects rather than objects.[1] The felt objection to manipulation lies here. People think: Why wasn't I treated with respect?

The welfarist objection to manipulation starts with the claim that choosers generally know what is in their best interests. We know our values. We know our tastes. We know what we like. When our choices are a result of manipulation, they may not promote our own welfare, precisely because we have not been put in a position to reflect and to deliberate, for ourselves, about the relevant variables and values. This is especially likely to be true if the manipulator is self-interested or ill-motivated.

From the welfarist point of view, manipulation is only presumptively disfavored. A benign, knowledgeable manipulator could make people's lives better and possibly much better. But under realistic assumptions, the presumption against manipulation is justifiably strong, because those who manipulate us are unlikely to be either benign or knowledgeable.

Some of the worst cases of manipulation involve trickery – covert or hidden influences on people's choices, compromising their ability to make reflective and deliberative choices. Deepfakes might well be manipulative; often they are. Manipulators use sludge to their benefit; they put friction in our way and hide important features of the situation. Manipulation can also occur when sellers enlist social influences, as in the Barbie Problem. When people buy goods that they wish did not exist, they lose time and money. Their lives may go much worse. Their freedom is at risk as well.

Manipulation can be a form of theft. Social norms should stand against it. In the most egregious cases, so should law.

---

[1] Fleur Jongepier and Jan Willem Wieland, Microtargeting People as Mere Means, in *The Philosophy of Online Manipulation* 156 (Fleur Jongepier and Michael Klenk eds. 2022).

ACKNOWLEDGMENTS

I have many people to thank. Robert Dreeson, my terrific editor, offered invaluable guidance and suggestions at multiple stages. Four anonymous reviewers provided immensely helpful comments from which I have greatly benefited. Sarah Chalfant, my agent, provided support and guidance throughout. Jared Gaffe, Tate Harms, and Tascha Shahriari-Parsa provided superb research assistance.

I have been working on these issues for many years. For valuable discussions and comments at various stages, I thank Oren Bar-Gill, Anne Barnhill, Jonathan Baron, Tyler Cowen, Elizabeth Emens, George Loewenstein, Martha Minow, Sendhil Mullainathan, Martha Nussbaum, Eric Posner, Lucia Reisch, Eldar Shafir, Richard Thaler, Mark Tushnet, the late Edna Ullmann-Margalit, and Adrian Vermeule. Special thanks to Bar-Gill, Reisch, Thaler, and Ullmann-Margalit for joint work and many discussions that greatly informed this book.

Thanks to Harvard Law School for valuable support. Thanks to participants in workshops at Queens College, Cambridge University for terrific comments and suggestions. Thanks finally to Oxford University, and in particular to the Accelerator Program, for valuable help in the essential, accelerated closing stages. In those closing stages, some of the relevant research was undertaken as part of the Accelerator Fellowship Programme at the Oxford Institute for Ethics in AI.

The book is dedicated to Sendhil Mullainathan, mentioned above, because he is an incredible friend and colleague, because he is full of fun, and because his mind is so alive that it makes everyone else's mind alive, too.

Acknowledgements

I have drawn on various papers here, including Fifty Shades of Manipulation, 1 *J Marketing Behavior* (2015); Manipulation as Theft, 29 *Journal of European Public Policy* 1959 (2022); Sludge Audits, 6 *Behavioral Public Policy* 654 (2020); The Ethics of Nudging, 32 *Yale J Reg* 413 (2015), and Brave New World? Human Welfare and Paternalistic AI, 26 *Theoretical Inquiries in Law* (2025). In all cases, there has been substantial reorientation and revision. I explored some of the issues here in *The Ethics of Influence* (Cambridge University Press, 2015), and there is an overlap, occasionally significant, between that exploration and this one. But the world has changed, more than a lot, and on some issues, my views have changed, more than a little.

INDEX

advertising
  affect heuristic, 33
  case studies, 6
  cigarettes, 48
  known interaction, 39
  subliminal, 22, 44, 46, 48, 143
affect heuristic, 33–4, 35
Amazon, 165
artificial intelligence (AI)
  ChatGPT, 14, 168–9, 172–5, 191–4
  Choice Engines, 167–71, 175–6, 191, 195
  Her (Jonze), 165–7
  impatience, 176–8
  Large Language Models, 168–9, 171
  manipulation of choice, 191–4
  manipulation, control of, 194–5
  planning and bias, 169–75
  present bias, 171–2, 178, 180–1, 183–5, 189–90
availability heuristic, 35, 155

Barnhill, Anne, 22–4, 35–6
Baron, Marcia, 38
Beauchamp, Tom, 15–16
Brandeis, Louis, 50
Brave New World (Huxley), 164–5
Bursztyn, Leonardo, 112–13, 116

Cambridge Analytica, 4–5, 165
confabulation, 9
Consumer Financial Protection Bureau (CFPB, US), 60, 63–4
Coons, Christian, 20

Darwall, Stephen, 154
deepfakes
  Alvarez decision, implications of, 75–6, 77, 78
  counterspeech, 74, 77–8
  definition, 71–2
  doctored videos, 74–5
  false speech, 73–4
  First Amendment protections, 74, 76–7
  libel, 76, 77, 78
  manipulative nature of, 71–2, 79
  private institutions, responses, 80–3
  property right to one's person, 78–80
  reputational harm, 76, 77, 78
  trickery, 76
  truth bias, 79
Denmark, 140
Department of Transportation (US), 59–60
Dodd-Frank Wall Street Reform and Consumer Protection Act (2010), 63
Dworkin, Ronald, 12–13

Facebook, 3–4, 35, 80–3
Faden, Ruth, 15–16
Federal Communications Commission (FCC, US), 60
flirting, 23

Google, 165
Gorin, Moti, 16

harm principle, 41
Hatch Act (1939), 122

Hayek, Friedrich, 42–3, 52–4, 135–6
Her (Jonze), 165–7
Huxley, Aldous, 164–5

Inadvertent falsehood, 9
Indonesia, 83
Instagram, 112–13

Jonze, Spike, 165–7

Krug, Steve, 131–2

Luguri, Jamie, 50–1

manipulation, definitions
 checklist, 35–6
 and choice, 19–20
 coercion, 6–7, 20
 cognitive System 1, 20–1, 33
 cognitive System 2, 21
 cognitive systems, targeting of, 21–2
 deception, 9–11, 14, 26
 definitions of, 12–17, 22–4, 25
 emotions, induction of, 23
 as influence, 19
 lies, 8–11
 as moral concept, 12
 situational justification for, 11–12
 trickery, 17–19, 22–3
manipulation, evaluation of
 autonomy and agency, 38–9, 66
 consent, 43–4
 democratic authorization, 47–9
 dignity and humiliation, 37–8
 roles, 39
 transparency, 44–7
 See also welfarism.
manipulation, illustrative cases
 advertising, 6
 affect heuristic, 33–4, 35
 anchoring, 34–5
 availability heuristic, 35
 default rules, 6, 31–3
 loss aversion, 28–9
 relative risk information, 26–8
 social media, 3–6, 35

social norms, 29–31
store design, 33
manipulation, right against
 compelled speech, 64–7
 dark patterns, 56–7, 61–2
 deception, legal consequences, 51–2
 deceptive defaults, 57–9
 decisional autonomy, 52, 59–60
 egregious practices, 63
 forfeiture of right, 52
 markets and information, 52–4
 overbreadth, 55
 right to privacy, 50
 "Time is Money" initiative, 60–1
 vagueness, 55
Meta, 3–4, 35, 80–3
Mill, John Stuart, 41
motivated reasoning, 9

New Zealand, 120
Nineteen Eighty-Four (Orwell), 164
Noggle, Robert, 24–5
Nolan, Christopher, 87
nudges
 active choice, 152–6
 agency, 127–30, 132, 142, 162–3
 autonomy, 154–6
 behavioral bias nudges, 142, 154–5
 behavioral public choice, 160–2
 choice architectures, 129, 131–7
 collective action problems, 141
 customary law, 136
 default rules, 132–3, 140, 152, 154, 159–60
 definitions, 99, 130
 dignity, 157–60
 educative nudges, 141–2, 152–4
 ethical concerns for, 134
 ex ante vs. ex post judgments, 146–7
 freedom, 136–8
 infantilization, 159
 market failure nudges, 141, 144–5
 paternalistic nudges, 141, 149–52, 154
 perfectionism, 145–6
 preferences and choice architecture, 147–8

nudges (cont.)
  present bias, 150–1
  regulatory design, 133
  spontaneous order, 133, 137–8
  target population of, 139
  transparency, 142–3
  uses for, 128–9, 130, 138–40

Obama, Barack, 177
Orwell, George, 164

The Prestige (Nolan), 87
properly nondeliberative decisions, 24–6

sludge
  Air Canada, 97
  cognitive scarcity, 87–9, 98
  dark patterns, 94
  data acquisition, 100–1
  distributional effects of, 98
  eligibility/qualification, 101
  excessive friction, 89, 91, 92–3
  Free Application for Federal Student Aid (FAFSA), 92
  inertia, 95–7
  institutional interests in, 104–5
  as nudges, 99
  opportunistic use of, 97
  opt-out provisions, 87–8
  present bias, 93, 96
  privacy, 99–100
  private sector, 91
  program integrity, 101–2
  public sector, 91–2
  qualitative forms, 92, 93–4
  security, 100
  See also sludge audits.
sludge audits
  benefits of, 90–1, 104
  dark patterns, 103
  Information Collection Budget (ICB), 105
  information forcing, 103–4
  proportionality, 103
  purpose of, 89–90

reforms, 103
TSA Precheck Program, 90
social media platforms
  Facebook/Meta, 3–4, 35, 80–3
  Instagram, 112–13
  policy reforms, 123
  TikTok, 112–13
  YouTube, 81
social pressure
  collective action problems, 110, 115–17
  consumer goods, 116
  fashion, 115–16
  fear of missing out, 107, 108, 111
  fundraising, 109–10
  goods, addictive, 119–21
  goods, bad, 106–7, 116–17
  goods, nonpositional, 118
  goods, positional, 118–19, 121
  joy of missing out, 107, 110
  loot box problem, 110–11
  norms, 117–18
  perceived disadvantage, 108, 114
  policy implications, 121–2
  product traps, 112–14
  social signals, 107–9, 110
  stag hunt, 115–17
Stolen Valor Act (2005), 73
Strahilewitz, Lior, 51

TikTok, 113

United States
  carbon tax, 189
  Consumer Financial Protection Bureau (CFPB, US), 60, 63–4
  consumer welfare, 179–80, 188–9
  Department of Transportation (US), 59–60
  Dodd-Frank Wall Street Reform and Consumer Protection Act (2010), 63
  Energy Paradox, 185–7, 188
  Federal Communications Commission (FCC, US), 60
  fuel economy mandates, 180–5

Hatch Act (1939), 122
Stolen Valor Act (2005), 73
"Time is Money" initiative, 60–1, 94, 105
United States v. Alvarez, 73–4, 78
vehicle labels, 178–80

Warren, Samuel, 50
Weber, Michael, 20
welfarism
  best interests, 40–1, 197
  context, 42–3
  democratic authorization, 48
  dignity, 158, 160
  education, 153–4
  eligibility, 102
  health warnings, 42, 66
  manipulation, 40, 41–2
  nudges, 129
  paternalism, 41, 149–52, 154
  transparency, 45–6
Wilkinson, T. M., 14–15, 43
Wood, Alan, 16

YouTube, 81